LEARNING
IN SAFE SCHOOLS

Creating classrooms where all students belong

FAYE BROWNLIE

JUDITH KING

Pembroke Publishers Limited

This book is dedicated to our children,
Levan and Gaby.
May they always experience warm and inclusive schools
where they feel secure and valued for who they are.

©2000   Pembroke Publishers
538 Hood Road
Markham, Ontario L3R 3K9
www.pembrokepublishers.com

Distributed in the U.S. by Stenhouse Publishers
P.O. Box 360
York, Maine 03909
www.stenhouse.com

We acknowledge the financial support of the Government of Canada through
the Book Publishing Industry Development Program (BPIDP) for our
publishing activities.

Canadian Cataloguing in Publication Data

Brownlie, Faye
   Learning in safe schools: creating classrooms where all students belong

ISBN 1-55138-120-6

1. Teaching. 2. Learning. I. King, Judith, 1954- . II. Title.

LB1025.3.B768 2000   371.1   C99-932891-3

Editor: Kate Revington
Cover Design: John Zehethofer
Cover Photography: Ajay Photographics
Typesetting: Jay Tee Graphics

Printed and bound in Canada
9 8 7 6 5 4 3 2 1

Contents

Introduction: Inclusion as We See It

There has been a move in the educational community over the past twenty years to full inclusion — the practice of educating students with special needs in the regular classroom as much as possible. We have witnessed the demise of special classes, the trepidation felt by teachers as their classes changed, and the renewed vigor that grows from collaboration in the classroom with a teacher and a support teacher working together to better meet the needs of all students. It is in this setting that we strive for practices that create a safe and productive learning environment for all.

We have moved from "allowing" students with special needs "in" to welcoming all students and working to build classroom and school communities where everyone feels a sense of belonging *and* makes academic progress.

What is inclusion?

- Inclusion is the practice of welcoming all students to their neighborhood school.
- It is the practice of educating all children in age-appropriate, heterogeneous classrooms.
- It is the practice of working together as a staff to better meet the learning needs of each and every student — whether or not a student has been identified as having special needs.
- And it is the practice of designing programs for children with special needs which rely, as much as possible, on the learning objectives and practices of the regular classroom.

Why value it in schools?

- Education is more than an academic process. We need to develop the brain *and* the emotions and to use children's strengths to build academic success.
- Schools provide the advantage of a community. We learn to move beyond a collection of individuals searching for their rights to a welcoming community which works and learns and feels together.
- Students with special needs learn so much from the modeling of their age-appropriate peers — both socially and academically.
- Non-identified students learn about acceptance and respecting differences. Everyone is reminded that we all learn in different ways and at different rates.
- The world is shrinking dramatically and constantly changing. Schools should reflect and prepare students for the best society we know — the one we want to help create. Surely this is one that respects and values all its members.

What are the core values and beliefs of *our* model of inclusion?

- All children can learn, albeit in different ways and at different rates.
- Learning is a developmental, active, continuous, constructive process, building on the prior experiences of the learners.
- All children can be included, have the right to be included, and may, indeed, challenge us on making inclusion a positive reality in the classroom and school.
- School should be a place where all students and staff enjoy a sense of belonging and a belief that they contribute. They should also feel valued.
- Teachers, students, administrators, and paraprofessionals will grow personally and professionally by working together to meet diverse needs.
- Successful inclusionary practices are possible, manageable, and happening in a variety of ways in a variety of places.
- Although a change to more inclusionary practice can be threatening to many, it does not mean taking time away from regular students, lowering standards, or allowing labeled students to "be there, keeping a seat warm."
- Children are the province of the whole school, not *one* teacher.

How do we begin to be inclusive?

- *Be flexible!* It is the most important characteristic needed by all staff. This flexibility will be called upon in thinking, in planning, and in designing support models. These models need to be dynamic, changing as learner needs alter. Listen to the voices of a few inclusive practitioners:

> In my first year here I had more resource room intervention which certainly took less of my energy because the kids left the classroom. Now with the resource support in the classroom, I need more energy but the results are well worth it.
>
> — Steve Rosell, teacher

> This inclusive school must have a community feel to it. It is a welcoming school, with a problem solving kind of atmosphere, where, when concerns, issues, problems develop, rather than throwing our hands in the air, we problem solve in groups of two or three or whatever. Maybe the key is flexibility. . . .
>
> What has also been critical is our supporting the classroom teacher. [re: a Kindergarten student who "loses" control] We have had to pull time from other kids and teachers in order to intensify the support for this situation. We talk together about supporting one another. Some teachers don't like it at first, but they also know that we'll be there for them when a critical situation arises.
>
> — Randy Cranston, principal/resource teacher

- *Be collaborative.* We truly need the expertise of all in order to make the move toward more inclusive practices work. Teachers, parents, and students can collaborate. We need to share our views, pose questions, and listen carefully.

  The best thing about collaboration is that adults learn from each other. It is an ongoing, connected inservice which involves modeling and reflection. This model has most helped one of the authors here refine her skill as a teacher.

  And another teacher, Tammy Wirick, observes: "The best thing about collaboration is that it forces you to question whether what you are doing is best for the children you are working with, and it provides a mirror — it balances your thinking both emotionally and intellectually."

- *Be prepared to problem-solve.* Each student can open a new range of possibilities. The whole school must be a safe place for everyone.

  Working with really challenging "behavior children," is worthwhile. As one teacher, Linda Wingren, puts it: "The other kids love you too because they see that you never give up on anyone and you include everyone. We can't afford to let go of anyone."

- *Be a planner.* Planning is key. Support personnel must work carefully with parents and classroom teachers to design appropriate educational experiences (to adapt the curriculum) on an ongoing basis. Plans are best established before support personnel join the teacher in the classroom. This does not have to mean a delay in service. Support personnel should be in the classroom early in the term, observing, collecting information, assessing student performance, scaffolding learning, and interacting with the students. Then, armed with pertinent information, the classroom teacher and the support personnel meet to establish their plans, which should be monitored regularly for service to be effective.

  Planning is nine-tenths of the program. One resource teacher, Gina Rae, says that when she and teachers meet "it is a very open process. We prioritize the needs of the class and then make a commitment to act. We plan one term at a time and renegotiate the timetable as we go. The teachers know it is not forever. I keep my timetable available for all the teachers I work with. This helps us be better as a group and helps create a school feeling for all the kids."

- *Be aware of the language used when describing students.* Choice of language is powerful. It influences the thinking of others — that of the students and their parents, as well as those who work with the students in school. Always refer to students in positive language. For example, saying "a student with learning disabilities" is more positive than saying "a learning disabled student." The first focuses on the student, then a specialty, while the second suggests that the disability is more important than the person.

  Stay away from labels. Labels prevent us from understanding students. They limit our ideas of who students are and what they can do. With our thinking falling into stereotypes, we then limit students' experiences and response. For example, how can a teacher call a child who isn't performing a non-reader and a non-writer? The task is to find out what is stopping the child and then figure out what to do about it.

- *Be aware of how you spend your time.* Extensive testing prior to providing a program for a student is costly in terms of time and personnel. Vulnerable students should not be left to flounder with the regular classroom curriculum and expectations pending a formal assessment. With support personnel helping the teacher in the classroom, observations of a student's interactions with others can begin immediately. These observations then become the nucleus of a profile of strengths and needs which lead to the necessary programming adaptations or scaffolding. Although a formal assessment may sometimes be required, most planning for student programming is based on ongoing data collection in a variety of learning situations. It is also tied to the curriculum learning outcomes and to classroom experiences. This planning is interactive and closely monitors a student's progress.

    "When I'm in the class I know I'm connecting to the curriculum that's being taught in the classroom," says principal and resource teacher, Randy Cranston. "I can scaffold for the students and teach them the necessary skills. . . . I also find the students are more motivated when their support occurs in the regular classroom."

- *If you are support personnel, be prepared to play a key role in beginning and maintaining an inclusive focus.* Accurate record keeping is a mandate. Ongoing dialogue among staff regarding student needs and the effectiveness of the intervention or scaffolding can often be initiated by support personnel. The modeling of positive language about students helps sharpen thinking. You are in a special position when it comes to influencing the growth of a learning community in a school. Remember: Inclusion is not focused on one population. It is making *everyone* feel that they are important and a part of the school. Behaviors ranging from welcoming to encouraging and from supporting to problem solving are all practised in a strong community. Students can capitalize on the social aspects of learning and, as members of a community, share the highs and lows of the individuals within it.

Why does the connectedness of the group matter?

The importance of inclusion, as advocated here, is eloquently summed up by teacher Kim Ondrik.

"I think of inclusion as being on a team. For some parents, all they want is for their child to learn more skills. I want the children in my class to benefit from being members of a team. This should develop their personal skills as well as their academic skills. There is a potential positive dynamic that exists in every group and this must be brought out and enhanced explicitly. The connectedness of the group is so important in creating safe, rich learning environments for everyone."

Part One

Building an Inclusive School

1

Developing a School-wide Code of Conduct

At our school we take pride in
- caring for and including others
- respecting people
- respecting and caring for property
- showing safety for self and others

— Draft, school code of conduct

Schools are complex places. Students, teachers, staff, administrators, parents, and often community members interact daily. Each school develops a particular culture.

Some schools let their culture develop on its own; other schools take steps to promote a culture that they value. In the latter instance, they seek to make the culture explicit to all members of the school community. One way of doing this is to develop a school code of conduct.

Developing a school code of conduct is a process. It is *not* just a matter of adopting another school's code. Some schools involve students and the larger school community in developing their code. If the staff believes that inclusion of all members of the school community is important, then they will invite those members of the community to take part. This invitation can be stated explicitly in the staff's philosophy that all belong, all need to be welcomed, and all have something to contribute. A school that wants to build this kind of culture will work through a time-consuming — but rewarding — process.

We recommend that a school code encompass all school community members. When you develop a code of conduct which *explicitly* states that all students, staff, and parents/guardians belong, then you have a strong foundation statement you can refer to when talking with students and adults about instances where certain members are excluded.

What follows is the process that one school used and the outcomes from that process. These outcomes are particular to that school. Another school using the process would develop a different set of outcomes.

Establishing the Process

In our school district, all of the schools were required to develop a school-wide code of conduct. The schools used many different processes: some involving staff only; some, staff and students; others, a wider group of people.

Our elementary staff decided to give everyone in the school community an opportunity to provide input into the school code of conduct. We decided to develop a long-term process that would take a year to implement and a lifetime to reinforce!

The teaching/administration staff met on a professional development day and looked at some codes of conduct that had been developed by other schools. Some were written in terms of rights and responsibilities; others, as short codes outlining behaviors.

We made three key decisions:

1. We wanted to develop a code which was meaningful, understandable, and easily referred to.
2. We wanted the students, parents, and non-professional staff to take part in the process in order to develop ownership of the school code.
3. We wanted to develop a process which was meaningful to all members of the school community.

We made the decisions knowing that having everyone involved in the process would encourage ownership. We believed that, if we were truly striving toward being an inclusive community, then all members needed to be part of establishing the philosophy and beliefs that would become the foundation for decisions made in the community.

We also recognized that involving more people would take more time.

Implementing the Process

1. *The Public Invitation*

   A school newsletter and a parent advisory council meeting invited parents to join with the students and staff at a school assembly to begin the process of developing a school code of conduct.

2. *The First Assembly*

   At the assembly, students sang "Common Thread," a song which emphasizes community, caring, and inclusion. Next, several students read poems that emphasized the importance of working together and building friendships. Two teachers outlined what a code of conduct is, using the metaphor of a puzzle. Each important aspect of a code was a part of a puzzle that made up a whole picture. Together, the puzzle would reflect what a code of conduct was, who should be part of it, what members should expect from other members of the community, and what the vision of a safe and caring place would be.

   As each puzzle piece was described, it was placed on the overhead projector. The completed puzzle was a school building overlapping a large heart shape (see next page).

Building a Code of Conduct

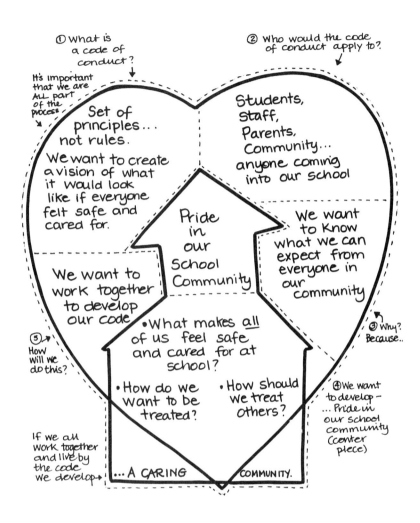

* cut on dotted lines - - - -

① What is a code of conduct?

It's important that we are ALL part of the process.

Set of principles... not rules.

We want to create a vision of what it would look like if everyone felt safe and cared for.

② Who would the code of conduct apply to?

Students, Staff, Parents, Community... anyone coming into our school

We want to Know what we can expect from everyone in our community

Pride in our School Community

We want to work together to develop our code

③ How will we do this?

•What makes all of us feel safe and cared for at school?

•How do we want to be treated?

•How should we treat others?

③ Why? Because...

④ We want to develop — ...Pride in our school community (center piece)

If we all work together and live by the code we develop →

...A CARING   COMMUNITY.

- At the end of the presentation, the two teachers posed this question to everyone: "What makes you feel safe and cared for at school?"
- With this question in mind, students, parents, and staff divided into groups of nine to twelve, each with an adult facilitator (teacher or parent). Each group was asked to brainstorm and record what made them feel safe and cared for at school. The session lasted ten minutes. If the brainstorming slowed, the teacher facilitators stimulated thinking through these questions:

> How do you like to be treated?
> How do you think you should be treating others?
> How should property and things such as books and computers be looked after?
> How do we keep ourselves and others safe?

What makes you feel good?
What does caring look like?
How would we want to treat adults coming into the school?

- Once response cards were collected, the students were told they would be doing further work with them in their classrooms. Parents were invited to meet in the staffroom with the principal to look at a variety of codes of conduct from other schools and to get a picture of what it was they were helping to develop.

3. *Classroom Work*
   - Each classroom was given approximately fifty cards. Their task was to sort and categorize the cards into five categories and come up with a name for each of these categories. The students were asked to try to develop at least one category name that no other group would likely come up with. The teachers found the strategy was successful with all grade levels.
   - The charts of categories were then displayed in the hallways.

4. *The Second Assembly* (one week after the first)
   - Students, staff, and parents again gathered in the gym.
   - The assembly opened with singing.
   - Each class presented their charts of categories and read out the five category names. Categories included Put ups, No Breaking Hearts, Friendships, and Things We Want.
   - The five categories from all of the classrooms were listed on the overhead and copies of this list were given to each classroom.

5. *Classroom Work*
   - Students worked to narrow all the category names to about five categories.

6. *The Third Assembly*
   - Students, staff, and parents gathered in the gym, opening the assembly with songs.
   - Each class presented their smaller list of categories.
   - Some of the older students presented scenarios of student behavior on the playground to highlight some of the category names that they had developed. For example, one group did a skit illustrating respect and disrespect for school property.

7. *Special Classroom Task*
   One intermediate classroom volunteered and took the category names and put them into the following general categories:

   respectful behavior — respect people
   respect property
   friendship — keeping friends
   no breaking hearts — including people
   things we want (safety)
   safety — a right to feel safe
   respect for our school
   helping

8. *Staff-Parent Meeting*

Staff and parents met to refine ideas further. They developed these points.

> At our school we take pride in
> - caring for and including others
> - respecting people
> - respecting and caring for property
> - showing safety for self and others

9. *Student and Parent Forums*

Students in all the classrooms and parents at a parent advisory council meeting took all the cards that had been written at the first assembly, to ensure they would fit into one of these four categories.

The full code of conduct then read as follows:

The _____ Elementary School community believes that it is important to establish a warm, supportive environment. We do this by:

- caring for and including others
- respecting people
- respecting and caring for property
- showing safety for self and others

Our code of conduct applies to all members of the _____ community. We use our code to teach and encourage positive behaviour.

Actions which do not respect our school code of conduct will result in appropriate consequences.

The final two lines were added because district policy required the inclusion of something of this nature.

The code of conduct was distributed widely. It was printed and posted around the school and put on large boards and displayed on the playground and on the outside wall of the gymnasium, where it could be seen by people visiting the school. Parents were sent copies through the school newsletter and were thanked for their involvement.

Reflecting on the Process

Having a code of conduct that was developed by the staff, students, and parents successfully encouraged ownership. Student voices were heard at each step. Adult input, as in the case of refining the final list of categories, was added only after the ideas had been developed by the students. If the final code was truly to reflect the philosophy of school community members, then it had to make explicit the foundation of beliefs of the school community. The code of conduct at this school explicitly reflects inclusion when it says "caring for and including others." This phrase gives students, staff, and parents something to speak to if they feel that they or other members of their school community are not being included.

Developing a code is only the beginning. Time, instruction, and discussion must accompany the code if students, staff, and parents are to live by the code. Keeping the code alive means calling upon the school community to reflect constantly on their beliefs and values — and then to "walk the talk."

Keeping the Code Alive

There are many ways to keep the code that took so much effort to develop alive. In this book, chapter 3 describes how to use the code as a teaching tool, and the Annotated Bibliography of Classroom Resources offers suggestions of materials and resources that can be used to help teach the code. Following are several concrete ways to reinforce the code and its values.

1. Set up monthly meetings of multi-age groups to do activities related to the school code. Possible activities are, as follows:
   * *illustrating each part of the code with different forms of art.* These representations can be displayed in the school or presented at assemblies.
   * *using the "pieceful strategy" to illustrate what each part of the school code really means.* For example, putting together a puzzle shape in the form of a heart represents "caring and including others"; putting together a puzzle shape in the form of a school building represents "respecting and caring for property." Again, these representations can be presented or displayed which makes the thinking behind the code more accessible for all students.
2. Hold monthly assemblies where classes take turns presenting role-plays, skits, songs, poems, and readings that bring to life parts of the code.
3. Use the language of the code explicitly in every situation. For example, when introducing a visiting drama group to a school assembly, you might say: "We'd like to welcome the Tropedoors, and show them how well we live by our school code by being a very respectful audience who will help them feel included in our school community."
4. Honor the parents, staff, and students who help to make the school a safe and caring place to be. When comments are made about the contributions of the noonhour supervisors, the custodian, the patrol parents, the office staff, and the library monitors, they are explicitly connected to the parts of the code of conduct.

5. Teach and reteach the code each year:
   - *Do T-charts.* Explore what respect for others looks like, sounds like.

RESPECT FOR OTHERS

Looks Like	Sounds Like
people listening to each other	Please, thank you
eye contact	I like your _____
holding open the door	That's a great _____
helping someone if hurt	compliments
taking turns	encouraging . . .

   - *Introduce carousel brainstorming.* Write each section of the code on different pieces of chart paper and have the students brainstorm what you would see if everyone in the school community was living by the code. If everyone was "showing safety for self and others," what would you see? A sample response for respecting property also appears below.

SHOWING SAFETY FOR SELF AND OTHERS	RESPECTING PROPERTY
going down the slide the right way	picking up litter
taking turns on the equipment	taking care of library books
	pushing chairs in
	asking before borrowing

   - *Develop People Searches.* Work with multi-age groups or individual classes. (See Appendix 1 for more on the strategy.) Ask students to find someone who can describe certain aspects of the school code. They might work with a form with directions such as these:

Find someone who
   - can tell you why we have a school code of conduct;
   - can describe a time when they felt they were included;
   - can tell you about a time when they helped someone stay safe;
   - can describe three ways they respect and care for property;
   - can imagine what it would be like if everyone in our school felt that they belonged.

- *Institute reflection journals.* Each week the students and staff can reflect on the code of conduct through writing or drawing. Here are some specific ways of jogging reflection.

Create a compliment tree for someone in the school community.
Draw a map of your heart and label the parts.
Collect data on the respectful language that students in your classroom use.
Write/draw four random acts of kindness you could try this week.

The following chart, "Summary of the Process Used in Developing a Code of Conduct," outlines the inclusive process we used for creating a code of conduct which will reinforce the desire for a safe school where all members of the community enjoy a sense of belonging.

Summary of the Process Used in Developing
a Code of Conduct

Staff met to develop process

|

parents invited to join staff and students
at assembly to introduce process

|

First assembly
songs and poems emphasizing caring and community
puzzle pieces used to describe what a code of conduct is
participants divide into small groups to brainstorm:
What makes you feel safe and cared for at our school?

|

classroom work
each classroom took approximately 50 cards
and sorted and categorized these cards into 5 categories
They named each category
charts were hung in the hall for everyone to see

|

Second assembly: one week later
songs
each class presented their 5 category names

|

classroom work
each class worked to narrow all the category names
down to 5 or so categories

|

Third assembly
songs
shorter list of categories were presented
older students presented skits to demonstrate some categories

|

one classroom
took all category names and narrowed them into
a short list of categories

|

staff
met to refine list further

|

parent meeting/classrooms
took original cards from first assembly and categorized the cards into
the refined categories to ensure all items would fit into one of these
categories

|

Final Code

|

teach/reteach
keep code alive

2

Developing a School-wide Behavior Plan as a Teaching Tool

"The plan is critical. A few years ago, I had a student with very aggressive behavior. We had written a formal behavior plan for him and when I had worried parents, I could refer directly to our plan. He was really a challenge, but we kept him. He needed to be in his classroom with really good behavior examples. He'd had some damaging experiences, was having a hard time, and needed to learn that he could be OK with other kids. He's still in our school, years later."

— Steve Rosell, teacher

Taking the time to develop a school-wide behavior plan usually happens when concerns about student behavior on the playground, in the halls, and between classes come to the fore. Staff talk about the issues, and administrators tire of having a long lineup of students in the office after recess and lunch.

We believe that schools should develop a plan before behavior goes out of control. Once a school code has been developed, developing a school-wide behavior plan is a logical next step. The plan will assist students in learning alternative behaviors and provide a meaningful way to reinforce the school code.

The philosophy behind the school-wide behavior plan, described in this chapter, is to educate students and the wider community on the variety of alternatives available. The plan is not in place as much to eliminate inappropriate behavior as it is to assist students in seeing that they have alternatives to their current behavior. It recognizes that students can choose how they act and react to others; they can learn to make positive choices and solve many of their own problems. The plan also involves working with parents to see issues or problems that their child is facing at school as an opportunity to talk with their child at home.

Our school-wide behavior plan also involves recognizing individual students and other school community members when they follow the code of conduct or solve problems in a positive way. When students go out of their way to welcome a new student to the school, spontaneously assist a teacher or parent, consistently show respectful behavior on the playground, or solve a problem independently, our plan recognizes them.

When a staff decides to implement a school-wide behavior plan, one of the critical aspects necessary for success is that all staff members agree on the reasons for and the implementation of the plan. We believe the plan is a teaching tool, not a punishment, so every staff member must not only agree, but philosophically understand what it means to work closely with students as they reflect on their behavior, regain their self-control, and make plans for a new start.

To demonstrate how a school might develop a school-wide behavior plan, we will share our experiences with the process.

Staff Development on the Theme

The school staff met on several professional development days to discuss and develop a plan for school-wide behavior.

On Day 1, a number of models used in other schools were introduced. Staff discussed beliefs and values about school-wide behavior, as well as ways to teach students to make positive choices and solve problems using words. They agreed to develop a plan which would use two forms to assist staff in teaching students to solve problems and in reinforcing positive student behavior.

At the second session, a half day, the teachers created the two forms. (See next page.) They brainstormed all of the behaviors that they considered fell short of the code of conduct and sorted the brainstormed ideas into the four areas of the code. They then discussed each item and ensured staff agreement on whether or not the problem-solving form would be used in these incidences. They did likewise with Form 2. Staff agreed on a process to be used in dealing with behavioral issues and the use of the forms. They developed a plan for how the forms and processes would be taught to the students and parents, how the forms would be distributed, and when a trial period should begin.

On the third occasion, staff role-played how to use the forms, focusing on the use of common language by all members of the school community.

At our school, we take pride in our Code of Conduct:

1. caring for and including others
2. respecting people
3. respecting and caring for property
4. showing safety for self and others

LIVING THE CODE

Student: _____ Class Teacher: _____

Date & Time: _____ Referred by: _____

Today I _____

_____

This is a problem because _____

_____

Some of my choices were (see over):

I could have: _____

_____

Dear Parents/Guardians:
Although there was a problem today, it is not our intention that this "Living the Code" sheet be a punishment. Rather, it is a means of helping children look at other behaviors they can use. We send it home so that parents/guardians will reinforce their child's appropriate behavior and talk with him/her about positive choices she or he can make.

Please sign and return this form to school. We invite you to respond on the reverse.

Thank you for your support. Please call (_____) if you have any questions.

Sincerely,

_____ _____ _____
    Student   Facilitator   Parent/Guardian

Form 1

At our school, we take pride in our Code of Conduct:

1. caring for and including others
2. respecting people
3. respecting and caring for property
4. showing safety for self and others

LIVING THE CODE

Our School is a better place because

_____

is Living the Code!

Class Teacher: _____ Date & Time:_____

Referred By:_____

Thank you for:

☐ caring for and including others
☐ respecting people
☐ respecting and caring for property
☐ showing safety for self and others

by: _____

_____

_____

_____

Dear Parents/Guardians:
We send this home so that you can talk with your child about the positive choices made. Thank you for your support.

_____   CONGRATULATIONS!
  Facilitator

Form 2

Living the Code Form 1 is used to assist adults who are working with students who need to take responsibility for their behavior and to help the students in solving their problems. Form 2 is used to reinforce and celebrate behavior that exemplifies the school code of conduct.

The process that the staff agreed to use with Living the Code Form 1 is outlined on the following page:

Summary of the Process for Problem Solving

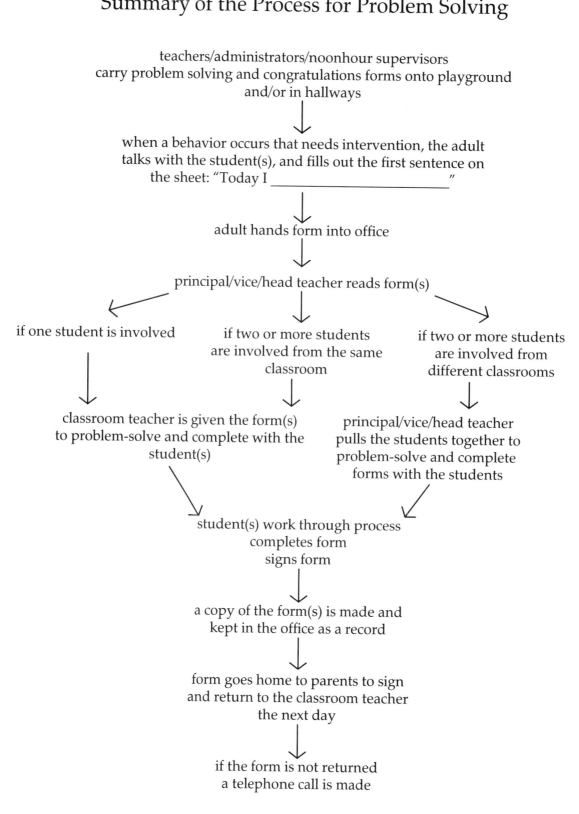

teachers/administrators/noonhour supervisors
carry problem solving and congratulations forms onto playground
and/or in hallways

↓

when a behavior occurs that needs intervention, the adult
talks with the student(s), and fills out the first sentence on
the sheet: "Today I _____"

↓

adult hands form into office

↓

principal/vice/head teacher reads form(s)

if one student is involved

if two or more students
are involved from the same
classroom

if two or more students
are involved from
different classrooms

↓

classroom teacher is given the form(s)
to problem-solve and complete with the
student(s)

principal/vice/head teacher
pulls the students together to
problem-solve and complete
forms with the students

student(s) work through process
completes form
signs form

↓

a copy of the form(s) is made and
kept in the office as a record

↓

form goes home to parents to sign
and return to the classroom teacher
the next day

↓

if the form is not returned
a telephone call is made

As reflected below, the staff agreed that a similar process would be used for Living the Code Form 2, the congratulations form.

Summary of the Process for Recognizing Positive Behavior

teachers/administrators/noonhour supervisors
carry problem-solving and congratulations forms onto playground
and/or in hallways
↓
when the supervisor notices a student who is living the code
the adult talks with the student and fills out
the entire congratulations form
↓
adult hands form into office
↓
principal/vice/head teacher reads form
↓
a copy of the form is made
and kept in the office in the code binder
↓
classroom teacher is given the form
classroom teacher congratulates student
and gives the student the form to take home
↓
form goes home to parents

Putting the Behavior Plan into Action

The staff agreed to and began to practise using a common non-judgmental language in problem-solving interactions. Teachers, administrators, and noonhour supervisors carry both Living the Code sheets with them onto the playground. Some use clipboards.

When someone notices behavior counter to the code, they intervene, saying something like "I can see you are having some difficulty. What is happening?" The adult listens to all sides, expecting that students will act respectfully toward each other. Students need to listen and not interrupt or show disrespectful body language. If they are unable to do this, then the adult should suggest they separate for a few minutes to cool down. The students should then be ready to talk about the incident.

The adult talks with the students and establishes agreement on what took place. She fills out the top part of a Living the Code problem-solving sheet for each person who's part of the problem. She may ask the students to separate, go to their classrooms, sit out of recess, or go to the office. She hands the forms into the office.

What an Adult Might Say to Two Students in the Midst of a Conflict

"I can't listen to both of you at the same time, so, we are going to take turns. One of you can talk first and say what happened from your perspective, then the other one will have a turn. It's your job to listen to each other. You can agree or disagree with the other person in your head, but you can't interrupt. When it's your turn, you can tell your story."

The principal, vice-principal, or head teacher reads the forms. If all the students are in the same classroom, the forms would go to the classroom teacher and she would discuss the problem with them. If the students are in different classrooms, the principal would see them, hear what happened, and assist in problem solving.

Here is a sample conversation.

Facilitator: So John, when you hit Peter, what part of the code were you not living by?

John: I don't know.

Facilitator: Let's read the code together and you see which part or parts you think hitting would go against.

They read the code together.

Facilitator: What do you think, John? Is hitting a way to show you care or include others? Is it respecting people or property? Or is it showing safety for self and others?

John: I guess it isn't safe.

Facilitator: Yes, I'd agree with you. It also isn't respectful or caring, is it? So let's fill in the next part of the form. . . .

At our school, we take pride in our Code of Conduct:

1. caring for and including others
2. respecting people
3. respecting and caring for property
4. showing safety for self and others

LIVING THE CODE

Student: <u>John Allen</u> Class Teacher: <u>Mr. Otto</u>

Date & Time: <u>Oct. 12/recess</u> Referred by: <u>Mr. Phillips</u>

Today I <u>hit another student</u>

_____

This is a problem because <u>it isn't safe and it</u>
  <u>isn't respectful</u>

Some of my choices were (see over):

I could have: _____

_____

Dear Parents/Guardians:
Although there was a problem today, it is not our intention that this "Living the Code" sheet be a punishment. Rather, it is a means of helping children look at other behaviors they can use. We send it home so that parents/guardians will reinforce their child's appropriate behavior and talk with him/her about positive choices she or he can make.

Please sign and return this form to school. We invite you to respond on the reverse.

Thank you for your support. Please call (_____) if you have any questions.

Sincerely,

_____ _____ _____
   Student   Facilitator   Parent/Guardian

*Note: The name of the other student is not used on the Living the Code form.

The facilitator helps each student in turn to fill out the form. Staff and student discuss alternative actions, creating a web of ideas. Should any suggestion be counter to the code, it is discussed and eliminated. Options deemed respectful and safe are circled and those that are not, crossed out.

Here is a web for the boy who hit another boy because he thought he was laughing at him.

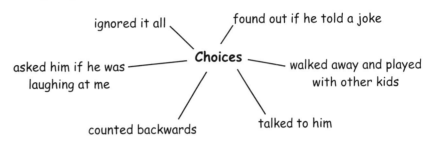

As part of exploring alternatives, a facilitator may ask students to role-play more positive behaviors. That allows students to see if the strategy has potential for them. The students eventually choose what seems to be the most viable strategy. For example, if they know they were too angry to talk, they might decide they would have been best to ignore the troublesome situation. The facilitator will ask students to reflect on what they have learned.

At the end of the meeting, students are expected to shake hands or ask for forgiveness. If they cannot do that, the facilitator will schedule another meeting. The completed Living the Code forms are sent home to be signed and returned by parents, while photocopies are made for office files. If, for some reason, a form is not returned promptly, a phone call is made.

There are, of course, exceptions to the rule. Sometimes children fear how their parents will react. The school respects such fears, either deciding against sending the form home, or phoning home first in an effort to allay children's concerns.

Schools that use the Living the Code process consistently have found that, over time, the children become more responsive and willing to discuss the issues, and much more adept at examining alternatives. The students soon learn that they have to solve their problems and come up with alternatives; they also realize that they have all the support they need to do those two things.

The other side of the equation is to recognize positive behavior. Teachers, administrators, and noonhour supervisors carry both Living the Code sheets with them onto the playground, keeping an eye out for student behavior that exemplifies the code. For example, a teacher might approach a Grade 6 student who is organizing games for some of the early primary students.

Teacher: Sean, I've been watching you during recess as you've organized these games for the Kindergarten students. It's been really neat to watch how you include all of them! You've got great organizational skills.

Sean: Thanks. I like playing with them sometimes.

Teacher: I want to give you one of these congratulations forms, as a small way of thanking you for making our school a great place to be.

Sean: Thanks, Ms. Jensen.

After such an exchange, the teacher would thank the student again, give the form to the principal to read, and ensure that it is delivered to the student's classroom.

Recommendations on Introducing a Behavior Code

Should your school adopt a Living the Code–type process, it is beneficial to have a trial period. When some schools introduce the process and forms, they have a trial month or two. They use the forms and follow problem-solving procedures, but the forms do not go home.

A trial period allows the staff and students to refine the process and experiment with how it will work. Role playing is done in the classrooms frequently so that the students understand how the process works.

A trial period also permits parents to become familiar with the concept. Parents are aware of the trial period and are invited to come to school assemblies and parent meetings about the process. Newsletters explaining the process are sent home before the forms begin to arrive there.

Keep in mind that the Living the Code forms are secondary. These forms can be used in any school and not really assist children in learning to solve problems or reflect on their positive behavior. They can easily be seen as reward and punishment — good kids/bad kids. The forms must be seen as part of a bigger picture, as tools for the development of students' social skills.

In order to truly use the two forms as teaching tools, the staff must visit and revisit the process they've developed. They need to reflect on the language they are using with students, and teach the code and the problem-solving process every day in their classrooms. This teaching can be both implicit in their dealings with students and explicit through class meetings, social skills training, novel studies, and songs.

If we want students to understand and internalize what we are teaching them, we, as a staff, will have to live and breathe the process.

3

Building a Culture Where All Students Belong

co-authored with
KIM ONDRIK
*with input from Rhonda Staples,
Deb Webster, and Lorraine Hanson*

"A seed holds an incredible life force. When conditions are right, the seed bursts, sending forth an embryo root and stem. Each time, the same thing happens with mind boggling regularity. *But the key to the process is to give the right seed the right conditions — which is the gardener's job.*"

— Gerald Knox, gardening authority

"From my belonging research I have learned that this simple idea is at the core of every person. It's the soil from which a seed grows . . . belonging is to learning as soil is to a seed."

— Kim Ondrik, teacher

Fostering a culture of "belonging" in a community can help children develop love, friendship, commitment, and caring. This "belonging" moves students to act in an inclusive way, change behavior, go out of their way for others, and appreciate others for who they are.

How deeply these changes happen in the classroom seems to depend on the individual teacher: how much the teacher cares about developing an inclusive culture, how able she is at reaching individual students, and how involved she allows the students to be in developing that community. Teachers who value a culture where everyone feels they belong set it as a priority, and constantly model respect and caring in their behavior and language. Many teachers believe, though, that a strong culture is more easily built when then have the same students for a few years.

The "Journey" outlined on the following page is an example of a teacher who cared about establishing a culture of belonging in her primary multi-aged classroom.

The Need to Belong as the Soil for Learning

The term "belonging" was coined by A. H. Maslow and appears with "love" on his hierarchy of needs. Maslow put forth the premise that human beings are motivated to satisfy needs. These needs are hierarchical and must be at least partially satisfied before a person will try to satisfy higher needs.

One critical concept introduced by Maslow was the distinction between deficiency needs and growth needs. Deficiency needs (physiological, safety, love, and esteem) are those that are critical to physical and psychological well-being. These needs must be satisfied, but once they are, a person's motivation to satisfy them diminishes. In contrast, growth needs, such as the need to know and understand things, to appreciate beauty, or to grow and develop in appreciation of others, can never be satisfied completely. In fact, the more people can meet their

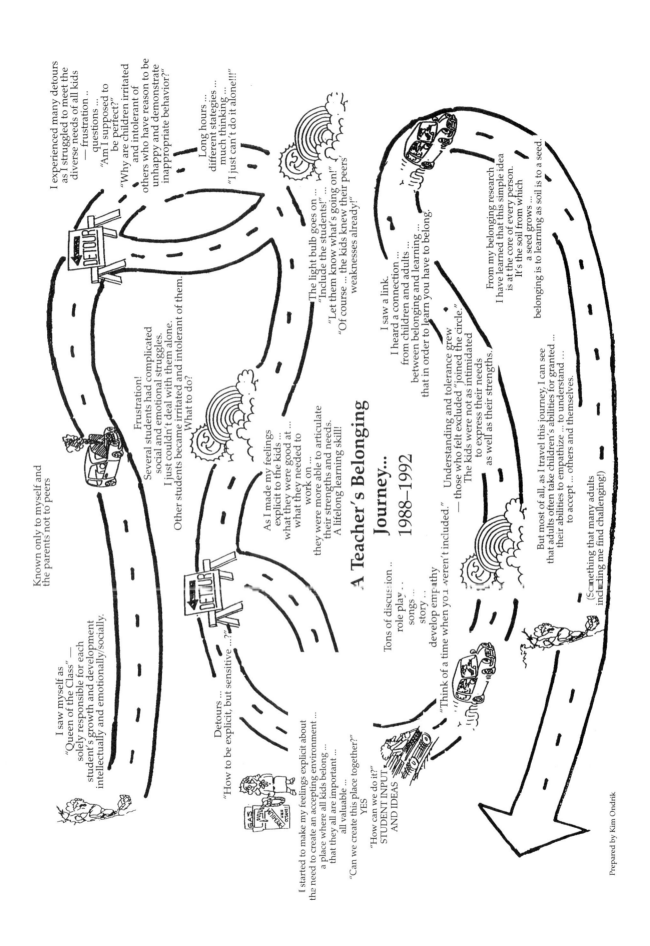

A Teacher's Belonging Journey... 1988–1992

Prepared by Kim Ondrik

need to know and understand the world around them, the greater their motivation may become to learn more.

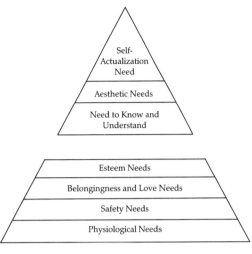

Maslow's Hierarchy of Needs

At school, we generally focus too narrowly on satisfying growth needs, developing children's intellectual skills. The problem is that children who are hungry or who come from abusive situations will have very little psychological energy to put into learning. They have many more basic needs to satisfy before they can grow intellectually. Similarly, if children do not feel accepted or included in a classroom, they are unlikely to have a strong motivation to achieve the higher growth objectives — the search for knowledge and understanding for their own sake, or the creativity and openness to new ideas. A child who is unsure of his acceptance in a class may feel sad or rejected, make the cautious choice, go with the crowd, or study for a test without any interest in learning the ideas.

If a teacher can create a classroom where all children feel they belong, in Maslow's view, the students will become eager to learn for the sake of learning. Children will also open themselves to new ideas and take creative risks. If they are to become self-directed learners, children must feel that they are loved, that the teacher will respond to them fairly and consistently, and that they will not be ridiculed or punished for honest answers or risk taking.

"If you belong, you learn more . . . you won't be worried."

— A primary class child

Classrooms built on the philosophy of belonging have caring, safe environments where children support and help each other. Such a philosophy promotes an "I can" attitude in all children. When children feel they belong, they feel safe and secure and good about themselves. As a result, they become tolerant of others, more accepting and forgiving.

Classrooms that foster a sense of belonging provide an environment which encourages risk taking, allows for a cooperative spirit, models acceptance, encourages divergent thinking, promotes appreciation of others, practises empathy, and recognizes the unique contributions that each individual makes to the group. Safe classrooms provide for effective exchanges between individuals. Safe classrooms are warm, loving, caring, and honest.

Establishing a Framework for Teaching Belongingness

Four understandings must be in evidence before the teaching of belongingness can take hold.

1. Make the concept explicit.

"Belonging" is a curriculum on its own. It has to be taught as life skills. It can't be treated as a theme that can be covered in a few weeks. This "belonging" curriculum has its own vocabulary that the children need to learn in order to communicate effectively.

"Belonging" should become a classroom word. Teachers need to talk about belonging with their students and bring the subtleties out into the open, letting the children become aware of what they do to promote it. Discussions centred around belonging make implicit social behaviors and feelings *explicit*.

The language of belonging is striking — love, care, value, important, share, help, encourage, friendship, support, freedom, choices, problem-solving. As students begin to understand the concept, their language becomes *descriptive* — "What does belonging feel like, look like and sound like?" Their language also becomes *prescriptive* — "What can you do so everyone belongs?"

2. Include children in problem solving.

Discipline problems are minimized when children understand the feelings of others and can better relate those feelings to their own experiences. In a classroom where belonging is emphasized, difficulties become everyone's problem. Everyone is responsible for the solutions. Fingers are not pointed and children are not singled out. Everyone works together to re-establish the feeling of belonging, giving the child ownership over the problem and a sense of empowerment from being part of the solution. By discussing belonging in the classroom, children's problem-solving skills are enhanced in a meaningful way.

3. Teach inclusion — and celebrate diversity.

Belonging allows for and celebrates diversity. A strong sense of belonging can transcend any unease created by diversity — physical, mental, and cultural. Talking about belonging and what is important helps children realize that it's their "heart condition," how they treat themselves and others, that matters, not how many toys they own, or how many different clothes they have, or how quickly they learn something new.

4. Establish a relationship with each child.

Children need a relationship with the adult in the classroom to get their bearings, to understand what is acceptable and not acceptable, to observe and emulate. They need to be able to transfer the relationship they have with their parents to their teacher, to know they are accepted, *safe*, and cared for. "Once there is a strong connection between adult and child, the child will respond to the tiniest cues from the adult," says child psychologist Gordon Neufeld. Penelope Leach, in *Children First*, writes that "Children depend on parents or their substitutes not only to maintain their self-esteem but also to build it." She believes that teachers need to play the role of the "parent substitute" and not be detached from students. She says further that teachers must be "involved in reciprocal interpersonal relations" with students, not see students as "objects to be taught if they will listen, controlled rather than consulted if they will not."

Concrete Ways to Create a "Belonging" Classroom

You can begin to create a genuinely inclusive classroom through discussions and activities, such as are outlined below.

1. Brainstorm "What is belonging?"

   We prefer to begin with whole-class brainstorming, moving to individual responses, which honor each child's contribution. An example appears below.

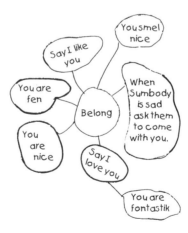

A place where I belong
is _____
because _____
A place where I don't belong
is _____
because _____

2. Ask students to reflect on where they feel they belong and why — and where they don't. This activity can be done using various formats at any grade level or using cross-grade buddies. One option is to provide open-ended sentences such as those at left above.

What does a classroom look like, sound like, and feel like where belonging is not thought about?

people that have hard harts and people don't make people Belong.

What does a classroom look like, sound like, and feel like where all kids belong?

3. Explore these two questions with your students: (1) What does a classroom look like, sound like, and feel like where all kids belong? (2) What does a classroom look like, sound like, and feel like where belonging is not thought about?

How One Primary Multi-Age Class Addressed Questions on Belonging

What does belonging look like in our classroom?	What does belonging sound like in our classroom?
• painting together	• come and play
• playing together (playground, swings)	• I like you
• going down the slide together	• I'll play with you. Do you want to play?
• making pictures, coloring together	• Do you want to come to my house?
• building something with friends	• You are a good friend
• sharing a book	• You have lots of detail in your picture
• helping me at cleanup time	• That is awesome
• working in groups . . .	• Thank you. You are welcome. . . .

What does it feel like when you belong?	What does it feel like when you don't belong?
• good	• scary 'cause I might get hurt
• warm and cozy	• sad
• comfortable	• hurt
• caring and loving	• anxious
• safe	• mad, angry
• fun and happy	• uncomfortable
• soft	• lonely, left out
• kind	• worried
	• like I'm in danger

4. Ask students to consider whether belonging helps them learn "school things." How does it do this? In a primary multi-aged classroom, the children seemed to connect *not belonging* to a preoccupation with problems that need to be solved, or with worry and anxiety. "If you don't belong then you worry." "If you belong, you get more

work done." "You can ask for help so you learn more!" "It's good to belong in the classroom because if you have a problem, you can't focus on your work — you keep thinking about your problem."

5. Invite students to respond to each triad of prompt statements below. They can tell their stories or draw their answers. See Appendix 2 for strategy.
   a) Think of a time when you belonged.
      Think of a time when you didn't belong.
      Think of a time when you made someone feel like they belonged.
   b) Think of a time when you weren't included.
      Think of a time when you saw someone not being included.
      Think of a time when you didn't include someone.

   Once through the process, pull the class together to reflect on what they learned from one another and how they can put these ideas into action.

6. Ask students to show, through drawing, when someone belongs and when they don't.

7. Every once in a while do a heart check and see how students are feeling about life in the classroom. This activity is a great starter for class discussions.

8. Introduce Thinking Yes, Thinking No to your students. Give each student a page divided in half. Ask the students to think of a time they felt loved, cared about, and included, then to think of a time they felt left out, alone, out of place. Before they begin their individual work, invite students to share some reflections with the whole class so they can get an idea of what others are thinking. For younger students who are new to the concept of belonging, you may connect the feelings of happiness and sadness to belonging and not belonging.

   The students draw and write about feeling included on the first half of the paper and share their thinking with a partner. Later, some students may share their reflections with the whole group. Repeat the process, having the students draw, write, and talk about not feeling included.

   After the children have finished the task, try to push their thinking. Ask them to describe why they felt the way they did. For example, "Kenny, what was it about going swimming with your friends and family that made you feel that you belonged?" or, "When the boy stuck his finger up at you, how did you feel? What was it about that that made you feel you didn't belong?"

   As the students describe specifically what made them feel they belonged or didn't belong, record their thinking in two columns:

Reflective "Heart Check"

Getting these ideas from my brain was ... great because
I just knew what
I was going to paint
in my head
I felt like I belonged today

in the class ♡ ♡

on the playground ♡ ♡ ◯

Happy or Belonging	Sad or Not Belonging
special time	alone
listened to	hurt feelings
somebody helped me	nobody cared

9. Make a large heart out of rolled paper, perhaps 1.5 metres (4.5 ft.) by 1.5 metres (4.5 ft.). Cut it up into jigsaw pieces so that there are enough pieces for each person in your room. Discuss with the students what makes them feel they belong at school or in the classroom. Give each student one puzzle piece to draw and write on. Have the class work together to make the heart shape. This heart can serve as a meaningful visual representation of what the class believes in and is working toward.

10. Have students write about their Belonging Journey as described in chapter 4.

11. Use literature to reinforce and spark further discussion about belonging and not belonging. For example, you might work with *The Very Best of Friends* by Margaret Wise and Julie Vivas.
    • Have the students predict the story from the title.
    • Choose four pictures from the book that show emotion, or examples of belonging and not belonging. Reduce the four pictures and copy them onto one sheet of paper. Make one photocopy for every two students. Have students work in pairs and cluster around the pictures their ideas about the pictures, or the story.

- Give the students four words from the story, for example: "lonely," "meowed," "snuggled," and "heart." Have the students illustrate the four words.

- Direct students to write a prediction of what the story will be about or a short story based on the book title, pictures and clusters, and the four vocabulary words.
- Read the story to the students. Stop in several places and discuss whether or not the characters are feeling they belong or don't belong. After completing the story have the students, as a group, gather evidence as to why the characters felt they belonged or didn't belong.

  One summary appears below.

Belonging	Not Belonging
they are together	cat had to stay outside
they love their cat	Jessie is alone in the house
the man and cat stay together	bolted the flap
the cat snuggles on the bed	William stopped doing all the familiar things
the man and woman snuggle	
the food bowl, flap in the door	cat scratches Jessie

- Read the story again. In the large group, invite students to identify and record heavy-hearted and happy-hearted words. Talk about the implications of using such words in the classroom and build a T chart of happy- and heavy-hearted words used there.

Happy-hearted Words	Heavy-hearted Words
loved, together, best of friends, happy, friends, pleased, snuggled, purred	alone, scratches, crossly, dreadful, cried, dark, lonely, yowled

An annotated bibliography of other suitable books is featured at the back of the book.

12. Create People Searches that focus on the concepts of belonging that you have been discussing. Directions for this strategy appear in

Appendix 1. You might ask students to find people who can do the following:
- imagine what a school would look like if all of the children felt they belonged
- name three ways they help others have a happy heart
- describe what cooperation means
- explain what "building other kids up" means
- tell you what belonging means to them
- explain why belonging is important to them
- remember a time they didn't belong

Find a researcher who can tell you . . .

People help Together (DIS)	because if People didn't belong They would be swallowed BRYAN
what belonging means to them	why belonging is important in life
at my other School	
when they didn't belong cristina	

When all of the students have completed their sheets, meet as a group and hear and discuss some of the answers. You may want to record some of the variety of answers on a master sheet.

13. Explore the theme of belonging through art, music, and drama. Have students create art projects that depict belonging or inclusiveness. An example of "rip art," done in red, blue, black, and yellow, appears on the following page. Students were asked to create a large picture representing what belonging meant to them, and to write on the art any words that helped to create the whole picture.

Teach songs and poems that focus on diversity, inclusion, celebration of differences, challenges, problem solving, and acceptance. *If You Could Wear My Sneakers* by Sheree Fitch is one example. You will find others in the Annotated Bibliography.

Use role-play and role drama to assist students in understanding and sorting through the dilemmas of tolerance, prejudice, friendship, and exclusion.

To me,
belonging means:

...seeing your strengths, and things you want to work on...

...warmth...

...having people share your thoughts, ideas and feelings with...

it's okay to be different

...being able to be yourself...

...having places you want to be...

...family and   friends...

...connecting - linking - joining...

...having support and encouragement...

Practical Ways to Help Parents Understand the Concept of Belonging

If we want parents to reinforce and extend the concept of belonging at home, then we need to provide parents with an opportunity to understand and experience what inclusion means. Parents need to know why the teacher is doing what she is doing, and be given an opportunity to ask questions, observe, and figure out belonging for themselves.

Teachers who welcome parents into their classroom for purposeful and meaningful reasons extend this feeling of belonging. These parents will experience first-hand some of the benefits of creating this kind of culture. However, just as it is important to teach the students explicitly, it is also important with parents. Teachers will need to articulate their philosophy to the parents and show consistent evidence of it through an open door policy. They will need to make personal connections and invitations, encouraging parents to be part of their child's education and classroom. Sending home informative newsletters and holding parent nights that model classroom culture are also constructive.

One teacher held a parent night and invited parents to come with their children. The parents were each given a People Search with questions about the culture of the classroom. For example, they were directed to find someone who could explain what belonging means to them, or could tell them three ways to include others. Parents were asked to move around the room, asking students to help them with the People Search. Not only did this put the children in the role of expert, it modeled for the parents what learning looked like in this safe and productive environment.

Reflections on Belonging

Explicit teaching of the concept of belonging opens dialogue in the classroom which enables students to talk about how they feel and allows others to care for them. It becomes okay to talk about personal feelings. Children can be heard reassuring others, such as in one case when a child said, "No one cares about me," and another six-year-old replied, "I do, Jesse, I care about you."

As students learn about and value belongingness, they become more articulate about what it means to them.

- "I like it when people listen to me, and when they listen I belong there."
- "I am a maker of friendships. I make places where everybody belongs."
- "I used to feel mad, sad, frustrated, . . . now I feel great because I can learn more because I belong."

Belongingness relates closely to emotional intelligence. Daniel Goleman has written that to him emotional intelligence is the true indicator of those who live rich and productive lives. He says emotional intelligence encompasses self-awareness and impulse control, persistence, zeal and self-motivation, empathy, and social deftness.

We believe that, in striving for classrooms where belonging is a given, teachers can enable more and more students to grow within their emotional intelligence. As a result, they can live — and learn — more productively, and our society will thrive.

4

Learning as a Journey

Co-authored with
KIM ONDRIK
*with input from Rhonda Staples,
Deb Webster, and Lorraine Hanson*

"Babies are born already pro-
grammed with a map of the long
and complex route towards matu-
rity and beyond, and with the drive
to travel along it. The route is the
same for every child in the world
but the scale of the map is too small
to show the millions of minor roads
and scenic routes, diversions and
disasters, roadblocks and resting
places that make each developmental journey unique with
unimaginable human diversity. Just
as a road map states total distances
between major cities but neither
predicts nor prescribes individual
journey times, so the developmental map is confined to neuro-
biological distances between
sequential landmarks. Babies cannot dance before they run, run
before they walk . . ."

— Penelope Leach, child psychologist

In this chapter, we present a whole-class strategy that will help students
to understand that we all have strengths and all have areas to work on.
Our goal is that children will honor their own strengths and needs and
the differing strengths and needs of those around them. We want children to realize that learning is a process, not a race. Learning and success can be defined without resorting to making comparisons.

To reflect the concept of learning as a process, we chose the metaphor
of a Journey. This concept links to the world outside the classroom because human beings are constantly learning new and different things.
We are all on lifelong learning journeys, each going at our own pace.

The Journey metaphor allows students to replace discussions about
"who's the best" with commentaries on "my learning journey in math" or
"my learning journey in cooperating." At times, students might make observations such as "I feel like a sports car when I'm learning reading," or "I
feel like a snail when I play soccer." Just as travellers take different modes
of transportation to get to where they want to go, the students will dis-
cover that all of their learning journeys are unique. Removed, then, are
the strong and damaging comparisons made between students.

When learning is seen as a journey, movement along the continuum
becomes the goal. Each student has a goal to keep moving on his or her
journey, whether artistic, emotional, intellectual, physical, or social. The
concept of learning journey acknowledges the strengths, needs, and development of every student — we all have things we are good at, and
we all have things we need to work on. It is important that, while on
their journeys, everyone moves along the continuum of development,
feels good about their accomplishments, and has some fun in the
process.

Classrooms that focus on learning journeys become communities of
learners who do not tolerate put-downs, sarcasm, or comments which
imply that because you are having difficulty you are stupid, and because you do it easily you are smart. Instead, they focus on encouraging
others to try again, lend a hand, cooperate, use personal strengths to
help others, and value and respect individual differences.

In order to create this type of classroom, the teacher must first embrace the idea that learning is a process and that all members of the classroom are on unique journeys. She then needs to focus on building a rich community where individuals help fuel each other's journeys.

Ways to Introduce the Concept of Learning Journey

Get your students thinking about learning journeys through many class discussions, small-group work, and individual reflections. Explore some relevant questions with them. You want students to realize that we learn some things very quickly, other things very slowly. What matters is the forward movement.

1. What is a journey? What words do we associate with journey? What happens on journeys? What are they like? Below is a web which an early primary class brainstormed.

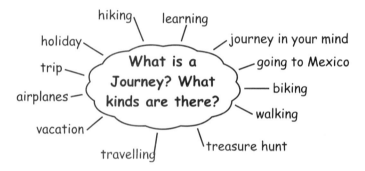

2. We know we look differently from each other. Do you think that we feel and learn differently too? Why or why not?

3. Are we smart at everything or slow at everything? What kinds of things are you quick to learn, and what kinds of things take you more time?

4. If you think of yourself as a lifelong learner, which matters more — speed or movement? Why do you think that?

5. How do you think we learn? Fast like a racecar, slow like a turtle, or at some other pace?

6. We are good at some things and need to work on other things. What is something you are good at? something you need to work on?

7. Since you are on a journey, consider where you have come from. Where do you want or need to go? Can you chart your journey in reading? in math? in soccer? Where were you in September, and where are you now? (This is the essence of reflection.)

Symbols That Relate to Learning as a Journey

We have found it useful to use symbols that connect with the metaphor of learning as a journey.

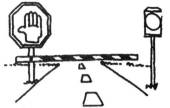

Roadblocks: What are the roadblocks on your journey? (i.e., reading journey, writing journey, cooperation journey, and so on) What do you need in order to get over/around them?

Fuel/gas station: What will help you to move on your journey? Is there something you need to learn in order to move? Do you need to be encouraged? Do you need assistance?

Uphill: What goals do you struggle to reach? How does that feel? How can others help you get up that hill?

Downhill: What goals have been easy for you to reach? How did that feel? Did others help you?

Carpool: Are you more able to move on your journey if someone helps you? But remember they can't do it for you!

Detour: Do you need to try something else before you can move on your journey?

Illustrations by Riffe Bauman

Beyond exploring many questions to raise students' awareness about learning journeys, plan to provide classroom activities that stimulate discussion and reflection on the topic. Several activities are outlined below.

1. Map out two adults' life journeys (e.g., yours and that of another teacher) on long rolled paper, using the same amount of space for each five years so that you will be able to compare and contrast the journeys. Note some similar events on the two journeys, e.g., first walked, talked, rode a bike, got first job, learned to drive. Then add other life experiences that were significant to each individual (first travelling experience, birth of a child, purchase of a new house, and so on).

   Display the two life journeys. Talk through each journey and point out significant events. Ask the students to compare and contrast the two journeys. In what ways are they similar and in what ways different?

   Look at some specific differences. For example: "Did you notice that Ms. Berezowskyj and I learned to drive a car at different times? I was 16 and Ms. Berezowskyj was 25. Is it okay to learn things at different times? Does it make me smarter than Ms. Berezowskyj because I could drive a car earlier? We all learn some things faster and some things slower. We all have things we are good at and some things we need to work on."

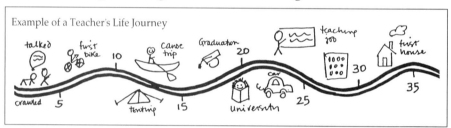

Example of a Teacher's Life Journey

2. Invite students to create their life journeys, noting some similar events (crawling, walking, talking) and then significant moments for them. When completed, whole-group and small-group discussions can take place, comparing similarities and differences among children. You can reinforce throughout the discussion the vocabulary and concepts you are trying to introduce: good at, working on, slow at some things, fast at others, it's okay to learn things at different rates, and so on.

Example of a Student's Life Journey

With a buddy, students can compare their learning journeys and record similarities and differences on a Venn diagram, such as is shown below.

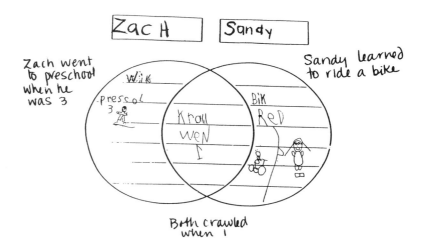

I am good at:

riding my bike without training wheels.

I am working on: SKATING

I learn fast like a go-cart.

3. Have students draw and write about things they are good at and things they are working on.

   For example: "I was fast at crawling. But I was slow at meeting friends."

4. Ask children to bring in photographs of themselves as babies (the beginning of their life journeys). Then they can reflect on their lives and create webs: "I used to . . . but now that I am seven, I . . . ."

5. Invite students to come up with similes in response to this question: "On your learning journey, how do you move?"
   Here are a few examples:

   I can learn slow . . . like a house tour, like a leaf, like a nail, like a tree trunk, like a brick.

   I learn like a cheetah. I can go fast if it's running and slow if it's walking. That's how I learn.

   I am journeying like a black tipped shark. I can learn slow, fast, and medium just like the shark moves.

   You will see that students readily relate to the idea of learning as a journey. As a result, they feel empowered to use this notion to describe, understand, and reflect upon their learning.

6. Students can apply the concept of learning as a journey to understand and reflect upon their own growth in all areas of their life . . . writing, reading, friendships, soccer. This ability to reflect and to then plan with the information gained is called metacognition, or thinking about your thinking. In a study of the past fifty years of research on learning, Wang, Haertl, and Walberg list metacognition as the second most important factor in helping students learn. (*Educational Leadership* 51(4))

Reflecting on writing journeys is very easy if students use a portfolio collection or a written journal throughout the year. At different points in the year, students can look through their portfolios or journals, note any changes in their writing, and mark these on a writing journey. To help them do this, begin by brainstorming the kinds of things the students might look for: BME (beginning, middle, end), connections to feelings and experience, elaborations on ideas, titles, more complex sentences, punctuation, and descriptive words. After making their journeys, they can set goals for the next term.

In reading, a similar brainstorm can be done.

7. After much discussion about journeys, you can try to map out a reading or writing journey with the students. Most students are not aware of the milestones involved in learning to read or write. Although they may be aware that they have progressed in their journey, they are probably not aware of what that journey entailed or when it began. For many students, you can either read or you can't read — it's an all or nothing endeavor. For some students, reading symbols such as the big M for McDonald's has absolutely nothing to do with "real reading." The following map, created by a class of seven- and eight-year-olds, reflects a deeper understanding of what constitutes reading.

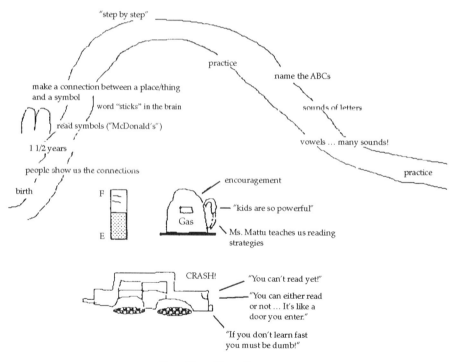

Our Reading Journey

"I learned that you do not have to be in school to be able to read and that you learn step by step."

— Student, age 7

"People read from symbols. You don't just step outside the door and read. It's a journey."

— Student, age 8

Many students, who have been struggling with reading and, consequently, low self-esteem because they believed that they couldn't read, may now gain a fresh perspective. Reading is not something that you can or cannot do. It is a process which begins at birth, and everyone moves at his own pace, in his own way.

Roadblocks

Fuel

fuel for my journey:

If I was having trouble reading, James could help me by telling me the word I was stuck.

8. Discuss the kinds of things that help or hinder people in their journeys. Talk about how each of us affects each other's journey. We might help others or hinder others by how we respond. For example, what happens if someone laughs at you when you are reading, or makes a comment like "Wow, you sure can't read!" How do those reactions affect you and your reading journey? And how do you feel when you are trying something new and someone says, "Good for you!" or "Wow, I sure like your painting!"

Introduce or re-introduce the symbols of roadblock and fuel tank. Brainstorm with the children ways that we help others by fueling up, and ways that we hinder or block others' journeys. Encouragement is fuel for the journey. When people encourage us in our learning, it makes us feel good about what we are doing, and then our brains can relax and learn. Saying something hurtful or discouraging can actually stop people from learning: the brain downshifts into a fight or flight pattern. Research is now indicating that threatening environments can even trigger chemical imbalances in the brain. As Eric Jensen says in *Teaching with the Brain in Mind*, these "threats activate defense mechanisms and behaviors that are great for survival but lousy for learning." Threats make a roadblock in the brain.

We talk with the children about hurting people's feelings without even thinking about the effect. People might not look hurt, but inside we may have hurt their hearts and put up roadblocks. Maybe we have stopped them on their friendship journey, running journey, soccer journey, or reading journey. We need to think about what we say and try to be encouraging.

Some questions and activities about fuel and roadblocks follow.

- What are all the ways you can give fuel to someone?
- Draw yourself giving fuel to someone in your class.
- Draw yourself trying to learn something that is hard for you and show what kind of fuel you would like to get.
- Make a personal web and show ways that others can help or hinder you on your journey.

Fuel for the Journey: A Kindergarten Class

Throughout our lives, people put up roadblocks for us. What can we do to help ourselves feel better and stay on our journey without becoming discouraged? Have the class brainstorm for ideas such as encouraging self, talking to a friend, engaging in positive self-talk, ignoring discouraging comments.

9. Review the journey symbols. (See page 43.) Give an example of a journey of yours to the students and talk about parts of your journey. Show where you had to struggle, what parts were downhill, where you took detours, etc. Have students make up maps of their journeys in many areas. They can use the symbols associated with journeys or describe the things that helped or hindered growth.

10. Explore journeys through literature such as *Thank You, Mr. Falker* or *Mrs. Katz and Tush*, both by Patricia Polacco, or watch a video such as *Homeward Bound*. Map out each character's journey and the ways that others helped or hindered their journey. See the Annotated Bibliography for additional selections.

11. Role-play and reinforce compliments, "put ups," and other inclusive comments. Doing this helps students reinforce and practise responses, enabling the positive to become more automatic. "If I am discouraged about my journey in soccer, what would you say or do? What could I say and do?"

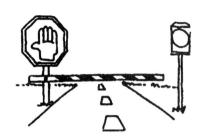

Doc Smith told Little Willy that grandfather doesn't want to live anymore and doesn't even want to go fishing or to the rodeo.

— Excerpt from a learning journey based on *Stone Fox*

Reflections on Learning as a Journey

Knowing the concept of learning as a journey is vital. Children need to understand this so they feel better about where they are. Development *is* a process and one that we are on forever, if we so choose. When students understand this, there is a new respect for their own learning processes and that of others. It will not be unusual for them to approach their teachers and parents asking them about the new things they are learning, or to hear children encouraging each other, "Keep practising, you'll get it."

As with many of the concepts described in this book, in order to be effective, the teacher must model both the language and the attitudes in her daily dealings with the students. If the teacher is expecting all students to do the same work and praises only those who complete it the best, the first, or the tidiest, she is not modeling what process and journeying are all about. If the philosophy of the class is based on competition rather than helping one another, then the idea of journey will not be realized.

The metaphor of learning as a journey fits philosophically within the context of safe, inclusive classrooms — classrooms built with collaboration, open-ended learning methodology, and respect for all individuals as they proceed on their respective journeys.

Part Two

Teaching So All Students Can Learn

5

Planning Lessons with the End in Mind

"In inclusive schools, the focus is not exclusively on how to help students . . . fit into the existing, standard curriculum of the school. Rather the curriculum in the regular education class is adapted, when necessary, to meet the needs of any student for whom the standard curriculum is inappropriate or could be better served through adaptation. Possibly the most common curricular modification in inclusive schools involves arranging for students to pursue different objectives within the same lesson."

— Stainback and Stainback, authors of *Support Networks for Inclusive Schooling*

All teachers can describe a lesson or a series of lessons which went extremely well — all students were included, all were engaged and learning, the outcomes of the lesson were being met. The challenge we face, however, is to teach such successful lessons often, not as rare highlights. We believe that a carefully crafted plan is fundamental to increasing the occurrence of "great lessons."

Teachers who are working toward a classroom where all students feel they belong begin their planning with the end in mind. They determine the key concepts or big ideas for the lesson or lesson sequence, the intended learning outcomes, and the ways students will demonstrate their learning. Then they plan the resources, strategies, and support necessary to help all learners achieve success.

Teachers who desire to take this approach may find the checklist on page 52 helpful.

Below we offer a viable model for planning for productive learning.

A Recommended Planning Model

What are the key concepts which the students are required to learn?

The first critical step is determining the key concepts — the big ideas, the major focus, or a purpose which guides the learning events. Once determined, the key concepts serve as a guide as the lessons unfold. Each activity that is then planned will help to make clearer to the students the big ideas.

What specific learning outcomes will be addressed in this lesson or lesson sequence?

Most curriculum guides today are written with learning outcomes clearly stated. It is not uncommon for there to be many more outcomes than

Checklist for the Teacher Who Values
an Inclusive Classroom

— Are my activities open enough so that all students can participate?

— Am I using various ways for students to build information and to demonstrate information?

— Are there opportunities for students to work alone, in small groups, and as a whole class?

— Are my literacy expectations such that most of my students can meet them with support?

— Am I varying the way I present material?

Will my sequence allow me time to interact individually with my students?

— How will I plan with my resource support teacher to help all students accomplish the learning goals?

— Will the students be active?

— Is there choice in either resources, demonstration of understanding, or complexity and abstractness for the students?

could be achieved by most students in the year. In planning, the teacher reviews the outcomes in the curriculum guide and *chooses* several on which to focus. Learning outcomes may be chosen from several curriculum areas, resulting in an integrated lesson plan. They further focus the lessons by adding specific information to the key concepts. Sometimes we choose four or five learning outcomes on which to build the lesson sequence. Building criteria with the students helps them engage more fully with the learning and more clearly understand the expectations of the tasks. We limit the building of criteria to two or three learning outcomes. These outcomes then become our major area for assessment.

How will the students demonstrate their learning?

Students will need to give evidence that they have achieved the learning outcomes and understood the key concepts of the lesson. Demonstrations of learning should require students to reorganize the material in some way and to connect it to information previously learned. They should also be varied — oral, written, graphic, pictorial, individual, group. Criteria for an effective demonstration can be developed with the students or can be given to the students. Working with criteria helps make explicit to all the expectations of the learning.

How will we assess student learning?

The criteria for success, established before the lesson begins, need to be always available and visible to the students. Teachers use these criteria to judge student products or demonstrations. Students should also be encouraged to assess their own work and to set goals for future learning. Two questions focus the students' attention:

• What do I need to know?
• How will I show what I know?

The key concepts, the learning outcomes, and the appropriate demonstration and assessment form the background for the lesson sequence. The next critical step is to paint the foreground. This involves examining the stages in the learning sequence and the type of *support* required at each stage to ensure all learners learn.

Learning Stage 1: Connecting

At this stage, the focus is on what is already known. Prior to the introduction of a new resource, a new topic, a different point of view, time is spent activating prior knowledge with students: predicting, questioning, writing to learn, sketching, examining specialized vocabulary, connecting the content with real-life stories, examining images or charts. This time of talk, small-group work, question posing, and connecting with self and others is critical to engaging the emotions of students, their curiosity, and their sense of personal relevance, all key factors in learning.

Learning Stage 2: Processing

The focus is on making sense of new information. Strategies at this stage teach students to think about the content being presented, to develop deeper understanding, to read or view interactively, to sort key ideas and align them with supporting details, to connect the new information to their previous understandings and to their questions, and to pose new questions. If students do not actively work with the information, it does not enter their long-term memories or become available for further use.

Learning Stage 3: Transforming or Personalizing

Once the information and experiences have been presented to the students, students need to gain ownership of them, to review and confirm what they have learned. This personal practice sets the students up to use the key concepts in the future and in different contexts. Strategies can include concept maps, drawings, role dramas, writing, or group presentations. Students use their new information to represent what they know in a different way. They work toward meeting the criteria for a powerful demonstration of understanding.

The Inclusive Nature of Adaptations

With this planning model, teachers assume that all students will be included. They design sequences and strategies that allow for a range of goal-directed responses. The atmosphere of the classroom acknowledges and honors each learner. Many students who might once have needed adaptations no longer need them.

However, there will still be some students who need adaptations. Consider the group plan: What is to be learned and what is the sequence to facilitate this learning? With this plan in mind, individual adaptations can now be preplanned and quite specific. Where does a given student require support or adaptation? In the environment? In the presentation? In the materials? In assistance? In the goals? In the evaluation? Some of the adaptations will be lesson specific, some more long-term.

Some students may require Individual Education Plans (IEP). An IEP takes into consideration the student's strengths and needs. The purpose of the IEP is to ensure the student is continuing to progress in the identified areas.

In inclusive schools, these IEPs are developed collaboratively between the classroom teacher, resource teacher, parent and, often, the student. They are working documents that guide actions. The IEP looks at ways to assist the student in his regular classroom, the place where he spends all or most of his time.

These IEPs are in contrast to the ones that used to outline in detail the child's pullout program, but did not usually deal with the larger period of classroom instruction time. The nature of the IEP reflects a school's commitment to the idea of inclusiveness. If one is to belong in a classroom and be included in a significant way, then collective actions must focus on this. This is the big idea of inclusion.

A Sample Lesson Sequence on the Concept of Belongingness

The following pages demonstrate the planning model outlined earlier in this chapter. Working with two key concepts, belonging, and the impact of our actions on others' feelings, the sample lesson sequence follows the thread from learning outcomes to the final stage of transforming. It shows how a classroom teacher can effectively engage learners of different strengths and abilities.

LEARNING OUTCOMES: Language Arts, Grades 1/2
Comprehension:
• make charts, webs, illustrations
• to organize information
• organize, with details
Engagement and Personal Response:
• connect thoughts and feeling to reading, viewing, listening experience
Composing and Creating:
• connect ideas and information to own experiences
• contribute relevant ideas to discussion
Presenting and Valuing:
• pride and satisfaction in using language to express ideas and feelings
Working Together:
• speak in turn
• listen actively
• willing to communicate ideas and feelings

Code for Assessment

+	beyond expectations
=	meeting expectations
^	working toward expectations

The teacher engages in personal planning so that she will be as prepared as possible to provide inclusive learning experiences through which students can learn productively with appropriate support.

The learning sequence that follows is based on use of the picture book, *Lilly's Purple Plastic Purse* by Kevin Henkes.

Day 1: Connecting

GRAB BAG: The Grade 1 and 2 students are seated in their table groups. In front of each student is an 11" x 17" paper, folded into four boxes. The teacher states that she is going to show them four artifacts from a story which they will read later. These artifacts all relate to the main character. As each artifact is shown to the students, they examine it, then draw how they think it will be used by or with the character in the story. The artifacts, presented one at a time, in the following order, are, as follows: (1) a red clicky-heeled shoe, (2) a sharp pencil, (3) a purple purse with three quarters, and (4) a large sign saying "The Lightbulb Lab Where Great Ideas Are Born." There is a wide range of student responses.

Dustin's second drawing

Emerald's first drawing

Kelsey's fourth drawing

One student, Dustin, begins with a boy wearing the red shoes and has him thinking, "I think I will do a tap dance." In his second drawing, the same boy with the tap dance shoes thinks, "Today I will write about my tap dance." In the third drawing, now including the purse, he thinks, "I will buy some food." Finally, in the last drawing, the Lightbulb Lab has him wonder, "I wonder what they are doing today." Dustin maintains the same character in each drawing, adds on each new artifact, and maintains the same setting, trees and sun.

Another student, Emerald, immediately connects the red shoe to *The Wizard of Oz* and draws Dorothy, the lion, the tin man, and the scarecrow. She adds thinking bubbles in which the lion admits his cowardice and Dorothy says she desires to get to the Emerald City. Emerald has not only connected with her background knowledge, but has added detail to her representation. In her second drawing, the woman wearing the red shoes is in trouble. A thief is running off with her pencil, while the chef yells "Fire!" In the third drawing, Miss Piggy, with her purse, is thinking of her money and wondering aloud what she will write to Kermit the frog, with her pencil. Again, Emerald has applied her prior knowledge and used all three artifacts. Finally, the lady, in her red shoes and with her purple purse, arrives at the door of a mad scientist. It is hinted that she will use her money to buy a "great idea." Emerald predicts, "There was a mad scientist who loved his lab and one day a very rich lady came . . ."

Finally, a third student, Kelsey, demonstrates a different form of thinking. Rather than work to integrate each new artifact with her budding theory, she makes an abrupt change in her thinking between the second and third artifacts. She began drawing and writing with Pasty the sheep having the prettiest tap dancing shoes in the whole pasture. A prospective customer awaits. In the second box, the pencils are included by adding another character — a magician, who gives Pasty some magic pencils for free. Now the major shift occurs. In the third drawing, Ms. Mulberry is wearing the red shoes and going out with her purple purse to buy pencils, being sold for 25 cents apiece. As she is walking home, in drawing four, Ms. Mulberry comes upon a sign for the Lightbulb Lab, so she goes in and gets a new idea.

All three students have connected the artifacts. All have worked to develop a plausible theory. The degree of sophistication varies; the engagement with the task does not. Dustin has met the basic demands of the task. Emerald has pulled extensively from her background knowledge, forming and abandoning possibilities with each new artifact. Kelsey has begun on one track, then shifted to a completely different theory.

Day 2: Connecting

WRITING FROM THE ARTIFACTS: The students are asked to write a story that includes all the artifacts they saw on the previous day. Dustin begins his story, but needs support in the form of scribing in order to finish. He begins with a known lead, "A long time ago in a far away land," then moves to rely heavily on the drawings he has already made and on the artifacts. However, when given the additional support of a scribe, his story becomes more sophisticated, though less tied to the artifacts.

Emerald continues thinking about the mad scientist. She uses all the artifacts, develops a conflict, and resolves it. She also employs conversation.

Emerald   DRAFT

Once upon a time ther lived a mad sintist He loved to werk with his labrotory then a stormy night a very very ritch lady came by oh thats just what I need a very smart bran and she walled into the lab and she didnot notes the sine but it said danger on it. Hm hm what will you give me if I give you a very smart bran now seed the very ritch lady. Haw ubout thows red tap dance shows oh no not my red dance shows my mother gave me those shows well haw ubout that pers oh no My tother gave me that pers well haw ubout those pensels oh no what will I writ with it I give you my pensels? Hm hm haw ubout the money well haw ubout that? So the very ritch lady got her very smart bran and the sintist got his money. The End

Kelsey changes her thinking again, as often happens over time. She, too, uses all the artifacts. Kelsey includes conversation, pulls in a dream sequence and in so doing, has a story within a story.

Day 3: Processing

PREDICTING FROM PICTURES: The students are working with partners. They share a large piece of paper, divided into four boxes. Each box has a picture from the text in it. The story is read to the students, stopping when the picture appears in the text. At this time, the students are invited to work together to decide what is happening in the picture and how the characters are feeling. This process continues for each of the four pictures.

Students' experiences are evident in their predictions. Two girls, Kelsey and Erin, predict that Lilly is drawing differently than the others — a cat, not a mouse — and that this returns to discourage her in box three. Emerald and Stephanie notice the rhymes on the board in the second box, then decide that Lilly is sad because her homework is not done. Dustin and Ben, again with help scribing, identify feelings with each picture, including the feelings of another mouse in box two: "He's mad at Lilly 'cause she gets all the good ideas, and she gets picked all the time by the teacher." Is this an experience with which they are familiar?

Day 4: Transforming

HAPPY HEART, HEAVY HEART: The students have now heard the book read aloud. Today, they focus on the three letters which Lilly, the main character, wrote to her teacher, Mr. Slinger. The book is reread, stopping at each letter in the book. The teacher guides the whole class by raising questions about the letters. (Copies of each letter can be shown on an overhead.)

Letter 1: Big Friendly Mr. Nice Man Teacher
    How was Lilly feeling when she wrote this?
    How will Mr. Slinger feel if he sees it?
    Which words are happy-hearted words?

Letter 2: Big Fat Mean Mr. Stealing Teacher
    How was Lilly feeling?
    How will Mr. Slinger feel when he gets it?
    Which words would make you feel you don't belong?
    How would you feel if you got this letter?
    Do you think Lilly should have given this to Mr. Slinger?
    Why or why not?

Letter 3: Lilly was really really sorry.
    How was Lilly feeling?
    How will Mr. Slinger feel when he gets this?
    Which words are happy-hearted words?
    How would you feel if you were Mr. Slinger?
    What do you do when you feel very very sorry?

In each case, the questions move from an examination of a piece of text to personal application in response to identified feelings. They help make explicit the feelings of the characters and of the students. This teaching allows students to develop a vocabulary appropriate for expressing their feelings and to appreciate the use of happy, not heavy, hearted words. Students will make strides in learning how to include everyone in a risk-free, productive learning environment.

Finally, the students, as a class, web A Happy Heart, deliberately focusing on how to act responsibly and how to have everyone in your group belong.

Happy-Hearted Words

"for you"
"me too"
lots
jaunty
saved
sharing
loved
special
wink
wow

Heavy-Hearted Words

hard time
not now
fierce
crying
gone
sad
longed
trouble

58

6

Making Adaptations and Modifications to Improve Learning

Co-authored with
RANDY CRANSTON
and
LAURIE MESTON

"We need to focus on instruction, not just on special education. I am always advocating for instruction and instructional change. We, too quickly, get caught up in labels and diagnosis and differences, rather than looking at how we are going to support learning."

— Randy Cranston, principal/resource teacher

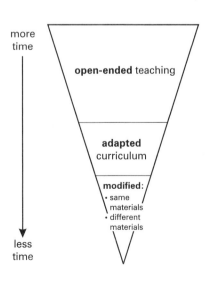

As noted in chapter 5, student learning is sometimes best served by making adaptations or modifications to the curriculum. An *adapted* curriculum maintains the same learning outcomes for the student, but may vary the goals/expectations, presentation, evaluation, materials, assistance, or environment. On the other hand, a *modified* curriculum is one in which the learning outcomes are different for the particular student, as identified in his or her Individual Education Plan. The materials used may be the same or different from those of the other students in the classroom. In inclusive classrooms, our goal is to have all students working with similar curriculum content and with similar materials.

The use of curriculum adaptation (over modification) where and whenever possible enhances the student's acceptance and inclusion in the classroom. It also reduces the amount of teacher time needed for planning and delivering multiple curricula.

When planning to meet the needs of a particular student, you may find the following specific questions helpful.

1. Which curriculum learning outcomes can the student meet without any changes?
2. What adaptations can be made, and where must adaptations be made for the student to meet these learning outcomes?
3. Which, if any, learning outcomes will need to be modified? (And can this be done using the same classroom materials?)
4. Are there any times when the student will be working on different learning outcomes with different, but age-appropriate, materials?

The order of these questions is important. Too often we have begun with the assumption that the child needs a separate curriculum. The overuse of a separate curriculum increases the exclusion of the child and the workload of the teacher.

It is very distressing to walk into a classroom and observe a child working on completely different packages of material, perhaps sitting with an adult helper, isolated from the classroom's social milieu. There is no chance in this environment to capitalize on the social interaction of learning. The student cannot follow the model of other children. He cannot learn from other students. He cannot observe and try to copy other students' behavior. Observing, often a strong learning strategy for students with special needs, is frequently the reason for being in the classroom in the first place.

Isolation is a picture too often taken of students who are designated English as a Second Language (ESL). How can we expect oral fluency when the language models are removed from new language learners and they are left alone with packages of primary phonics worksheets?

One ESL consultant, Vicki McCarthy, notes: "All of these ESL students come to school with at least five years of language — which is a huge amount of cognition and skills to be able to transfer. It is unfair to ESL students to assign them basic language exercises and not put into practice what we know about the social aspect of language acquisition. ESL teachers serve their students much better if they work together with the classroom teacher, in the classroom as much as possible, combining content expertise with curriculum adaptation expertise."

Ways of Adapting Curriculum

If you need to adapt the curriculum for certain students, there are many ways of doing it. These adaptations can be placed in the following categories: (1) goals/expectations, (2) presentation, (3) evaluation, (4) materials, (5) assistance, and (6) environment.

In the following section we are going to outline some ideas for making adaptations in these six categories. Other ideas can be found in the chart at the end of the chapter. Many of the ideas found in this chart have been brainstormed by teachers at in-service sessions. These ideas help teachers think creatively about ways to assist students in their classrooms.

1. Adapting Goals/Expectations

One of the most common adaptations is to adapt the goals or expectations for a child. This can be done easily and does not require a lot of pre-planning. For example, a child who has difficulty with fine motor skills could work on the same learning outcomes, but do every second question.

There are many other ways of adapting expectations and goals. Some of these include calling for smaller amounts of work, reducing the number of concepts to be learned, selecting concepts that relate directly to the student, simplifying or extending the work, using high-interest books, removing time constraints, asking a student to read the introduction, summary, and main titles rather than the whole text, and allowing alternatives for the way knowledge can be presented.

2. Adapting Presentation

The expectation in the classroom is that the teacher would make a general presentation of material to all students. However, some students might receive additional, adapted presentation. Consider these two questions: (1) What are the key points to remember when presenting effectively to the entire class? (2) What adaptations in presentation do I need to make for individual students?

Some ideas to think about when planning for presentation to the whole class include demonstrating and modeling the task (I do it, we do it, you do it); using graphic organizers to assist students in understanding how different concepts connect; building criteria with students so that they understand what they are working toward; using rhyme, rhythm, songs, patterns, and drama as alternative ways to present materials; using the overhead as you present so that students hear and see the materials being discussed; putting directions in the same place on the blackboard each day so that students know where to look for clarification.

When thinking about adapting presentation for individual students, we look at choosing strategies that make the greatest difference to student engagement and thus to learning. Some students require the presentation to be simplified or the directions broken down into a number of steps; others need specific hand signals or sign language; some might respond best to having parts of the directions in their text highlighted or underlined. For some students, just standing close to them when giving the directions might be enough, or, putting your hand on their shoulder might help them to concentrate on the directions given.

3. Adapting Evaluation

Beyond the standard test format, there are many ways of finding out what a student knows. There are both exemplary group evaluation practices and individually appropriate practices based on student need.

Some group practices include developing criteria with the whole class and then basing evaluation on those criteria. Once students understand the criteria they can do self-evaluation. Many teachers also use portfolio assessments and have students set goals each term, chart progress, and evaluate themselves.

Adaptations in evaluation will take into account students' special needs. Some students might require a scribe for answering questions. This support is often given in cases when the teacher is evaluating knowledge in a certain skill area such as social studies: the teacher wants to know if the students understand the concepts. A student with writing difficulties may understand the concepts, but may be unable to communicate it in writing. With a scribe, the teacher can better evaluate the student's knowledge in this area. Other adaptations in evaluation include reading test questions orally to a student who has difficulties in reading and having a student who has difficulties in writing draw answers or record them onto a tape.

"[Students in the classroom] start to extrapolate the idea that everyone learns in different ways and at different rates, that we can all still be kind to one another, and that we are all better at some things than others. We are all better prepared for life beyond school and accepting that differences are natural."

— Cynthia Higgins, special education assistant

4. Adapting Materials

Not all students need to use the same materials all the time to achieve the same learning outcomes. Most students can learn well using common classroom materials. However, for some students, a better materials match can significantly change their ability to learn.

In many schools, students who have difficulty with writing due to fine motor ability are using computers in the classroom. Doing this has helped students with note taking, organization, and the ability to read back what they have written. Some students with visual impairments or with fine motor difficulties have benefited from having materials enlarged. Other students find it helpful if their notebooks or paper are adapted slightly. If a student has difficulty lining up numbers in mathematics, often the use of graph paper is helpful. Students who have printing and writing difficulties can work with paper that has raised or enlarged lines to print or write more clearly.

Sometimes, students benefit from the use of adapted devices, such as left-handed scissors, pencil grips, erasable pens, or recipe stands to hold books or single sheets upright. Students who have difficulty organizing materials often benefit from the use of highlighters, or color-coded notebooks. Students with specific difficulties in reading or math might find it helpful to have a number line or alphabet taped to their desk. Other students have a personal dictionary to assist them when they write. Many of these adaptations are very small, but can make a big difference to a child's success in the classroom.

5. Adapting Assistance

Our premise is that the support teacher is working in collaboration with the classroom teacher and knows all the students in the classroom. The responsibility for the programming for students rests with the classroom teacher, in conjunction with the support teacher. These teachers consult each other, plan together, problem-solve, and jointly strive to teach every child well. If a paraprofessional is provided to assist, the paraprofessional should work to support the classroom program, whenever possible — not be attached to one particular student.

When you decide to provide assistance to students, move from the least adaptation to the most. For example, begin with a peer buddy in the classroom or an older peer tutor before requesting assistance from a paraprofessional.

A peer buddy in the classroom can assist another student in many ways: as a model, helper, organization assistant, reader, scribe, questions answerer, and tutor. Older tutors are often trained to assist students in academic areas. They might read to students, run through flashcards, or scribe a story.

Sometimes it is beneficial for the student with specific learning or behavioral needs to be a peer assistant. Many times, the student with specific needs benefits more from helping than from being helped! Such students may help younger students in math, reading, or centre time. They might also assist by being a library monitor, a score keeper, or the attendance collector for the school. When making decisions about appropriate tasks, be sure to look at each student's strengths.

Teacher assistants, as paraprofessionals, are assigned to a school or classroom to work with a whole class. Although they work in a classroom because there are students with specific needs, they follow teacher direction and assist all of the students in the classroom. Support teachers work closely with the classroom teacher to co-plan, co-teach, and problem-solve. They, too, work with all of the students in the classroom.

In some classrooms, teachers invite assistance from consultants, itinerant teachers, parent volunteers, and high school and university students. In all of these cases, the guest is under the direction of the teacher, and the assistance and support given students is invaluable.

6. Adapting Environment

For most students, almost any classroom environment filled with student work and teacher-prepared charts is okay. However, some students require adaptations to the environment to increase their success. Some students also need different environments within the day to enable them to focus during the time they are in the classroom.

A student who has difficulties concentrating on a task might benefit from sitting close to the teacher's desk, or working at a study carrel in the classroom during different parts of the day. Some teachers have a number of carrels in the classroom as an option for any student who wants a quiet place to work. Students who have difficulties seeing board work or the overhead benefit from sitting near the front of a classroom. Students who need to see the teacher speak or read lips should be seated close to where most of the directions are given, and away from glaring lights.

A student who can't readily concentrate for long periods of time sometimes benefits from working in several environments. Some students have timetables that require them to be in different places to do different jobs. For example, after thirty minutes of math, a student might be expected to go to the Kindergarten classroom and read with a younger buddy. Later that morning, he might be expected to help deliver notices in the office or work for a short time in the library. Adapted timetables are very useful for students with behavioral difficulties.

What follows next are some typical adaptations and modifications of curriculum.

Examples of Curriculum Adaptations and Modifications

Math, Grade 5: The focus is on long division. Many of the students are working on practice questions independently, several are working on the same questions with manipulatives, one student has an enlarged sheet because of her challenge with fine motor skills, and another student is working with a teaching assistant on the same questions. These are all *adaptations* in materials, presentation, and assistance.

One child is working on a *modified* curriculum. He is using the same division sheet, but working on a different learning outcome: to identify the numbers from 1 to 10. In this case, his task is to circle the numbers 7, 8, and 9 on the long division sheet. Thus, he is using the same materials, but is working toward a completely different learning outcome.

Math, Grade 2/3 combined: The focus is on measurement. Children are building with Lego and tangrams according to architectural briefs which outline the measurements required. All students are working in pairs or small groups. These groups have been teacher selected to ensure that all children will be successful. For example, there is a reader in each group, and in some cases, children who require more support are paired with students who can explain and assist so everyone can be successful. This setup exemplifies *adapted* assistance.

For two students this task is too easy: the students have already achieved these learning outcomes. They are invited to participate with the rest of the class but can opt to meet individual learning outcomes: one making an individual booklet on problem solving, the other constructing architectural designs on the computer. These are examples of *modified* programming.

Language Arts, Grade 6, Readers' Workshop: All students are reading books of their own choosing, responding in writing to their books, and meeting in small groups to share their responses. The learning outcome is to connect personal experience with text and thereby deepen text understanding. Two students are listening to their book on tape and often draw rather than write their responses. They sometimes summarize what they have read orally, or are prompted with "What does this remind you of?" They, too, are included in the small-group discussions. This is an example of *adapting* assistance, materials, and evaluation.

Planning for All Students in the Class

When planning a unit of lessons, the classroom teacher decides on the appropriate learning outcomes for the class and the ways that the students will demonstrate their understanding of these learning outcomes. The classroom teacher and support teacher then decide which of the learning outcomes can be met by all of the students, and which students will be at risk without some adaptations and/or modifications.

With the specific students in mind, the classroom teacher and support teacher can make adjustments to the learning outcomes (goals/expectations), the way the students will demonstrate their understanding (evaluation), or the presentation, materials, assistance, or environment.

The following example outlines learning outcomes for a Grade 3 class in Social Studies. It then shows two formats for writing classroom-based

Individual Education Plans, outlining the adaptations or modifications for two students.

LEARNING OUTCOMES: Grade 3 Social Studies Unit on Mapping
- Create and interpret simple maps using cardinal directions, symbols, and simple keys.
- Identify and describe major landforms and water bodies in B.C. and Canada.
- Identify and locate B.C. in Canada, North America, the Pacific Region, and the world.
- Identify and locate the provinces and territories of Canada.

Adaptations for Sam Using a Program Analysis Worksheet

Sam is a very able student orally, both receptively and expressively. She has no difficulty learning new concepts. She can read few sight words. She can print her first name and random strings of letters. She enjoys being in school and works hard.

Although Sam can meet some of the learning outcomes related to mapping, she needs some adaptations in order to be successful. As seen on the Program Analysis Worksheet (next page), Sam needs to have a peer read her the directions. She also needs an enlarged map on which to print and a reduced number of items to print on her map. In addition to the adaptations, Sam is working on some individual learning outcomes during this unit of study. Some of these include printing her first and last name, reading and recognizing "British Columbia," and increasing her reading vocabulary.

The Program Analysis Worksheet is fully explained on page 67. Easy to use, it serves as an example of a working classroom-based Individual Education Plan.

PROGRAM ANALYSIS WORKSHEET

©Cranston/Meston, Maple Ridge

Name: Sam
Curricular Area: Social Studies

Date Initiated: Sept. 29/99
Review Date: Dec. 5, 1999

Class Learning Outcomes • highlight appropriate objectives	Evaluation	As is	IS IT APPROPRIATE? with adapted goals/ expectations, presentation, evaluation, materials, assistance, or environment	Person Responsible	Individual Learning Outcomes (materials, criteria, review date)	Evaluation Comments (date achieved)
1. create and interpret simple maps using cardinal directions, symbols and simple keys	• ongoing data collection	✓	• partner with reader for reading of legends, keys, labels and map directions • use atlas as a guide	CT peer CT peer	• put first and last name on all papers • read and recognize British Columbia • increase recognition of province/territory names (to 5)	
2. identify and describe major landforms and water bodies in B.C. and Canada	• culminating activity		• provide symbols to match landforms as necessary • enlarge materials as necessary	CT CT	• increase reading vocabulary • point to N, S, E, W on map • share her knowledge in oral discussions	
3. identify and locate B.C. in Canada, North America, the Pacific Region, and the world	• ongoing data collection		• reduce the number of items to put on map	CT		
4. identify and locate the provinces and territories	• culminating activity		• reduce number of oral directions needing to respond to when reading response required. EVALUATION: Create a Map: have peer/ adult read key with landforms to Sam. Provide names of 5 provinces/territories to cut and paste. Interpret a Map: participate with rest of class. CT adjusts pacing of directions so all kids can follow. • focus on cirectional concepts, not recognition of place names • while class does challenge activity, check to see if there is a need for further evaluation of her knowledge. If needed, provide word recognition cues for place names.	CT peer CT CT		

66

How to Use a Program Analysis Worksheet

See Appendix 3 for a reproducible.

The Program Analysis Worksheet is used to adapt and modify the learning outcomes for a unit or theme. Typically, it is used for a student who can meet some of the classroom learning outcomes, but requires adaptations/modifications to be successful on all the learning outcomes.

The following steps provide a structure for using the Program Analysis Worksheet to develop and implement a plan that focuses on including the student in the classroom program.

1. List the class learning outcomes in the left-hand column. Learning outcomes can be cut and pasted from overviews, IRPs, and curriculum guides. Highlight any learning outcomes that the student can meet without any adaptations or modifications.

2. List evaluation methods/culminating activities for class learning outcomes in the Evaluation column. Highlight any evaluation processes that are appropriate to the student.

3. List any individual outcomes for the student in the appropriate column. These could include outcomes related to the curricular area or those that are more focused on behavioral/social needs, e.g., share knowledge in oral discussions or increase length of time on task.

4. Now that you have the classroom and individual outcomes listed, hang on to the individual outcomes as you develop ways to adapt or modify the class learning outcomes.

5. Examine each class learning outcome and ask yourself the following question: Can the student achieve the learning outcome if I adapt/ modify the goal, presentation, evaluation, materials, assistance, and/ or environment?

6. For each learning outcome, write general adaptations or modifications that may work for the student: for example, reduce the number of items required, complete every second question, partner with a reading buddy, enlarge materials where needed, dictate answers on a test.

7. Use these general adaptations/modifications listed as a guide to adapt specific strategies and activities to support the student's learning. (These specific adaptations could be noted in the teacher's day book beside the strategy or activity.)

8. Determine who will be responsible for the adaptations or modifications: the classroom teacher, peers, the support teacher, the teaching assistant, parents, or volunteers.

9. Complete the Evaluation column as the student meets the learning outcomes or at the end of the unit/theme.

Adaptations for Larsen Using a Program Analysis Worksheet and a Critical Activities Matrix

Larsen is able to verbalize about ten words. He can recognize the numbers 1, 2, and 3. He is working on making appropriate sounds at appropriate times, sitting with a partner, and staying with the group for whole-group activities. A paraprofessional is in the classroom most of the day to provide assistance.

Larsen cannot meet the class learning outcomes independently or with minor adaptations. Larsen's plan needs to be based on his individual learning outcomes. Some of the goals that he is trying to meet are verbalizing a greater number of words, increasing his use of appropriate sounds, identifying and matching colors, following simple directions, recognizing sequences of 1, 2, 3, 4. All of these individual learning outcomes can be worked on in Social Studies using classroom-based materials and resources. Larsen can work in small groups or with a partner with the same materials, but with different goals and expectations.

Two formats for Larsen's Individual Education Plan could be useful. One is the Program Analysis Worksheet; the other, the Critical Activities Matrix. This matrix is most useful for students whose learning outcomes differ significantly from those of their peers. It is fully explained below.

How to Use a Critical Activities Matrix

See Appendix 3 for a reproducible.

The Critical Activities Matrix can be used instead of the Program Analysis Worksheet. This form allows the teacher to integrate the student's individual learning outcomes into the classroom structure so that she or he can see where the child can participate in the daily classroom activities/routines. Such participation promotes acceptance and inclusion and encourages all involved not to automatically use parallel programs.

The following steps provide a structure for using the Critical Activities Matrix to develop and implement a plan that focuses on including the student in the classroom program.

1. List individual student learning outcomes in the left-hand column. Typically, these outcomes are not subjects, units, or specific themes, but the goals that the teachers/parents/students have set.

2. List daily activities or unit/theme strategies and activities across the top of the matrix. You can follow the plan of the day, or group some subjects together.

3. Connect each learning outcome with each activity. Think creatively. Plan with a partner. Ask yourselves questions, for example, "How can a child learn to identify and match colors during most periods of the day?" Then begin to brainstorm ideas — some will work, others won't. Could the child have color-coded notebooks? Could he or she hand out papers that are filed in color-coded file folders? Could each period of the day be color coded on the class agenda? Could rooms in the school be color coded and the child match attendance sheets to the room color? Could their cubby be colored? Could you use green and red marks for start and stop in a

PROGRAM ANALYSIS WORKSHEET

©Cranston/Meston, Maple Ridge

Name: Larsen
Curricular Area: Social Studies

Date Initiated: Sept. 29/99
Review Date: Dec. 5, 1999

Class Learning Outcomes • highlight appropriate objectives	Evaluation	As is	IS IT APPROPRIATE? with adapted goals/expectations, presentation, evaluation, materials, assistance, or environment	Person Responsible	Individual Learning Outcomes (materials, criteria, review date)	Evaluation Comments (date achieved)
			GENERIC ADAPTATIONS - Can be used for a number of the learning outcomes:			
1. create and interpret simple maps using cardinal directions, symbols and simple keys			• pair with a buddy wherever possible, particularly in activities where he can imitate actions	peer	• increase number of words he can verbalize	
			• Larsen will be materials manager in group activities	peer	• increase use of appropriate sounds at appropriate times • identify and match colours	
2. identify and describe major landforms and water bodies in B.C. and Canada			• Larsen will imitate initial sounds in words, e.g., names of landforms, names of provinces	SEA	• identify and match common classroom furniture and objects	
			• adapt paper/pencil mapping activities to focus on matching and labelling of colours and cutting and pasting	CT	• increase length of time on task (e.g., staying with group)	
3. identify and locate B.C. in Canada, North America, the Pacific Region, and the world			• participate, with adult support, in preparation of class activities when cutting, pasting and/or colouring are involved	SEA	• increase independence in cutting with scissors • increase independence in pasting on paper	
4. identify and locate the provinces and territories			• focus on concrete objects during mapping activities, e.g., classroom map, cutting, pasting, etc.	SEA	• follow simple directions	
			• enlarge materials as necessary	SEA	• recognize in sequence 1, 2, 3, 4	
			Evaluation: focus on individual not class learning outcomes	CT		
			Create a Map: match and label colours, identification of objects by pasting pictures of objects on a classroom map or matching colours on a map of Canada	SEA		
			Interpret a Map: on the pilot's route - prenumber the route so Larsen can participate by joining the numbers with a line	CT		

CRITICAL ACTIVITIES MATRIX
© Ives/Meston, Maple Ridge

Name: Larsen   Date: Sept.29/99   Review Date: Dec.5/99

CLASSROOM ACTIVITIES

INDIVIDUAL LEARNING OUTCOMES	Arrival	Silent Rdg/L.Arts	Recess/Lunch	Math	Music PE Art	Social Studies (Map)
Increase the number of words Larsen can verbalize	"Hi ___" "Hello"	"Reading Now" Handout books "___'s book"	"outside" "eat"	"one" "two" "three"	"cut" "paste" "red" "yellow" (Art)	"scissors" "glue" "help"
Increase use of appropriate sounds at appropriate times		Use quiet picture signal		Initial sounds of 1,2,3	• hum with music • cheer in PE	• initial sounds of N,S,E,W,
Identify and match colours	• colour coded cubby • Match colour on agenda	• colour coded notebooks ← (handout coloured coded note-books to coloured tables)		• colour coded book		• match colour to province/territory colour code name and map
Increase length of time on task		partner with buddy	encourage play with others	receive 1,2,3 cards before moving to next task	materials manager for small group	• must stay at activity for set amount of time
Increase independence in cutting and pasting		• cut out 10 words he knows, paste in book - read to a buddy		• cut out #s 1,2, 3,4 paste in approp. place	Art—Collage - cut, paste	• cut out labels & paste on enlarged map
Follow simple directions	Take cards 1,2, 3,4 put beside class agenda	• hand out materials • Give to ___	"get coat" "eat lunch" "close door"	• hand out materials "Give to ___"	"Line up" "come here" "cut"	"cut" "paste" "put here"

variety of situations? The list goes on and on. Using 11" x 17" paper helps to provide more space for writing a variety of ideas.

Adaptations are vitally important if children are to succeed in school and belong in the regular classroom. Many of the adaptations that we do for children are simple; others are more complex. Plan to develop any necessary adaptations with someone else: we have learned that that will make the job easier and the outcomes more creative. A summary of ways to make adaptations to improve learning begins on the next page. You can use these ideas to stimulate thinking and assist you in coming up with new ideas.

Summary of Ways to Make
Adaptations to Improve Learning

*Adapted from Maple Ridge School District,
British Columbia

These ideas were brainstormed by teachers at a variety of workshops.

Adapting Goals/Expectations

- Decide upon smaller amounts of work, odd or even questions.
- Reduce number of concepts to be learned.
- Select concepts that relate to student.
- Simplify/extend the work.
- Emphasize functional tasks.
- Use high interest books.
- Remove time constraints/extend time.
- Read introduction, summary, and main titles vs. whole text.
- Have alternatives for the way knowledge can be represented.

Adapting Presentation

Strategies for the Whole Class
- Demonstrate and model (I do it, we do it, you do it).
- Use graphic organizers.
- Build criteria with students.
- Be explicit about expectations.
- Give oral instructions from different places in the classroom.
- Use rhyme, rhythm, songs, patterning, drama for presentation.
- Keep in mind length of teacher talk (primary 5–7 minutes; intermediate 7–12 minutes).
- Modify pace — speak more slowly or more quickly.
- Encourage students to make eye contact with presenter.
- Break information into steps.
- Write down instructions.
- Always put directions in the same place.
- Use pictures.
- Use different color chalk/pens.
- Use overhead.
- Use multi-sensory examples.

Adapting Presentation — *continued*

- Give structured overview; students fill in the blanks while listening.
- Use two-column notes.
- Involve students in presentation — concept mapping.

Strategies for Individual Needs
- Use hand signals/sign language.
- Separate visual/auditory information.
- Repeat instructions.
- Preteach vocabulary.
- Stand close to student.
- Ask student to repeat the instructions.
- Have peer repeat instructions.
- Use concrete materials.
- Videotape for later review.
- Complete first example with student.
- Simplify instructions.
- Provide additional time to preview materials, complete tasks, take tests.
- Tape-record instructions.
- Highlight key points in textbooks — student just reads these points.
- If student has visual impairments, use high contrast materials and determine where and when they can see best.

Adapting Evaluation

- Self-evaluation.
- Peer evaluation
- KWL — **k**now, **w**ant to know, **l**earned
- Show knowledge in different ways.
- Develop criteria with students.
- Use different criteria to evaluate.
- Keep work samples.
- Portfolio assessment
- Do spot checks.
- Set small goals.
- Use video.

Adapting Evaluation — *continued*

Tests
- Use a scribe.
- Oral test.
- Have someone read test questions.
- Test on modified objectives (highlight questions student needs to answer).
- Use calculator.
- Draw pictures.
- Take test home.
- No time test
- Open book
- Provide more space to write.
- Delete some of the options.
- Take test in another room.
- Enlarge print.
- Tape test directions/questions.
- Tape-record answers.

Reporting
- Give work habit grade/comment.
- Attach anecdotal comments.
- Use same format for other students.
- Use * to note modification.
- Focus on growth.

Adapting Materials

- Dictate to a scribe.
- Tape-record answers.
- Draw pictures.
- Cut pictures from magazines.
- Dioramas, build a model
- Laptop, computer
- Handheld word processor (like a laptop)
- Handheld translators
- Use overhead transparency sheets, paper clipped to the textbook pages, so student can write answers to questions in the book.
- Use manipulatives.
- Use calculator — talking type, larger size.
- Use colored pens to record thinking at different times.

Adapted Devices
- Scissors — have many types available
- Chalk holders
- Pencil grippers
- Highlighters

Adapting Materials — *continued*

- Bingo markers to indicate choice
- Date stamp, number stamps
- Dycem, Velcro
- Corner pouches to hold pages down
- "No-carbon-required" paper (NCR)
- Number line, alphabet on desk
- Erasable pens
- recipe stand to hold books upright, or single sheets
- vegetable bins to hold materials at table

Adapting Page Set-up
- Line indicators
- Different types of paper
- Paper with mid lines
- Raised-line paper
- Paper with red and green lines
- Provide more white space to put answers.
- Highlight directions.
- Cover sections of text/sheet.
- Provide greater contrast: blue ink is hard to see.
- Extra large print
- Work on bigger paper.
- Use Post-it notes to create text for pictures in reading materials.

Adapting Assistance

Support Teacher
- Consultation
- Supports teacher to teach every child well
- Work primarily in classroom with teacher
- Problem-solves with teacher

Peer Assistant
- As model
- As helper
- As organization assistant
- As questions answerer
- As reader
- As scribe
- As peer tutor

Peer Assistant (Student with Challenges)
- Helps younger student in reading, math, or general assistant. Look at student's strengths.
- Helps in school: office, library, cares for plants, score keeper, hands out books, sharpens pencils

Adapting Assistance — *continued*

Teacher Assistants (Paraprofessionals)
• Assigned to school, to classroom, works with whole class
• Facilitates ownership by classroom teacher and follows teacher direction

Consultants/Itinerant Teachers
• Work in classroom.
• Model for teacher.
• Use curriculum as guide.

Community Support
• High school students
• Volunteer grandparents
• Parent volunteers

Communication Tools
• Homework books/student planners
• Back and forth communication books

Adapting Environment

Classroom Environment
Position in Room:
• Consider student's senses: vision, hearing, smell, touch.
• Sit at front or back of room.
• Sit away from noise (lights, street, hall, computer).
• Use carrel/screens.
• Sit with back to window.
• Sit by teacher.
• Manage lighting (light on desk, back to window . . .).

Cooperative Grouping
• Seating at desk
• Wheelchair accessible desk
• Laptop desk
• Lip on side of desk
• Flip-up-top desk
• Tilt-top desk
• Use larger table instead of desk.
• Have student stand at desk instead of sitting.
• Use light box to work at.
• Provide box for feet so they are supported.

Adapting Environment — *continued*

General Organization
• "Lazysusan" to organize desk
• Drawers beside desk
• Soup can for pencils
• Bookends/bookholder to hold books on desk
• Tie pencil to desk.
• Attach pencil to student with extension key ring.
• Have list of items to complete on desk.
• Have timetable on desk, in notebooks (pictorial or written).
• Have student goal on desk.
• Reduce excess paper and materials on desk.
• Color-code class duotangs.
• Have student come in ten minutes early and go over day plan.
• Use headphones to quiet outbursts.
• Sit on mat at circle time.
• Sit on chair at circle time.
• Create legitimate opportunities to move.
• Designate places in the classroom for quiet time, special materials.

Different Environments
• Have student assist in another classroom for short periods of time, e.g., help teach PE to a primary class, stack chairs for the Kindergarten classroom, read to a younger buddy, or do a job in the office or library.

Part Three

Taking "Ownership" of All Students

Creating a Resource Model

The movement toward full inclusion of students with special needs into regular classrooms precipitated teachers examining their roles. Class-room teachers began to say, "I can't meet with all these different re-source people about students in my classroom." The classroom teacher might have to meet with many different resource people: the learning assistance teacher, the English as a Second Language (ESL) teacher, the reading teacher, the counsellor, teachers of the learning disabled, hear-ing impaired, visually impaired, behaviorally disordered, mentally chal-lenged, and multiply handicapped, and the nurse. Teachers were becoming overwhelmed by the resource contacts.

Many resource personnel also began to question the effectiveness of their roles. A learning assistance teacher might have forty-five children on a case load and twelve classroom teachers to consult with. Many learning assistance teachers would say: "I'm only bandaging," "I have no time to talk with teachers," "There is no carryover to the classroom."

Resource people began to compare roles and wonder how they could assist each other. For example, in schools where the teachers of students with learning disabilities might work with ten children, and the learn-ing assistance teacher might work with forty-five children, discussions began as to whether or not they could combine their resources and share the load more effectively.

The Move toward a Generic Resource Team Model

Many teams now work generically. The time allotted to the school for ESL, learning assistance, high incidence (learning disabled, behavior, mildly mentally challenged, gifted and talented), and low incidence (e.g., mentally challenged, more severe behavioral difficulties, multiply handicapped) is combined and used to hire teachers and special educa-tion assistants who can work with all students — those with identified

Resource Team Staffing

learning assistance	.7
ESL	.7
special education (low incidence, behavior, etc.)	.5
gifted/talented	.1
Total Teaching Staff	2.0

special needs *and* all the other students in the classroom. There is a philosophical shift when you make this move to a generic model.

At left is an example of how you might staff a resource team. The school begins by looking at the amount of staffing they are given and adding all of the time allotments together. For example, it might have the equivalent of two full-time resource teachers. In some districts, it may have the flexibility to make choices such as 1.5 teachers and a full-time teaching assistant.

Where there are two full-time resource teachers and fourteen classes, the resource teachers may choose to organize their service delivery in some of the following ways:

- Each teacher has seven divisions.
- One teacher is responsible for primary, the other for intermediate.
- The teachers may look at the needs of each classroom and decide that one teacher will have six divisions because there are more needs, while the other teacher has eight.
- They may look at their own expertise: the teacher with more expertise in ESL might take the classes with the greatest number of students who are new Canadians; the teacher with more expertise in behavior might take the classrooms where there are more students with behavioral challenges; the resources teacher who has strengths working with new teachers might take the classrooms with new teachers.

In all cases the resource team would meet weekly to share their expertise, ideas, and concerns.

The Evolving Roles of Resource Teachers

A resource person following the noncategorical model works very closely with classroom teachers in trying to meet the needs of *all* of the students in their classrooms. This collaboration is easier to manage in a noncategorical model because each resource teacher's time is devoted to fewer teachers. Instead of trying to talk and plan with every staff member, the resource teacher has a limited number of teachers with whom to work closely.

The role of a resource teacher who works noncategorically looks quite different from that of the categorical special education teacher (e.g., learning assistance teacher, ESL teacher, or reading teacher).

Unlike the traditional resource teacher, the teacher who works noncategorically tries to help all the students in a classroom, not just specific referrals. The teacher works with some classroom teachers to adapt and modify the curriculum for a wide range of students, as well as to design ways to assess and evaluate. He or she may co-teach, co-plan, work with a larger group while the classroom teacher meets with a smaller group, and supervise parent volunteers or a peer tutoring program.

While traditional special education teachers gave a battery of assessments and wrote lots of special programs and report cards, resource teachers now write individual reports on classroom-based adaptations in collaboration with others. They observe students regularly and use assessment techniques that connect with the classroom. No longer are individual students routinely pulled out of the classroom.

Service Delivery as a Reflection of Inclusiveness

Noncategorical resource teachers work collaboratively with the classroom teacher to meet the teacher's and the students' needs. How they might do this is limited only by the teachers' combined creativity. The following menu describes in detail some of the roles a resource teacher might take.

Menu for Resource Teachers

Co-planning with the classroom teacher is essential in all of the roles that a resource teacher plays, whether service delivery is in the classroom or in the resource room. The teachers must communicate in order for the child's program to be connected in meaningful ways.

A. Co-teaching

1. The resource teacher and classroom teacher may schedule in weekly blocks of time when they teach together in the classroom. This can look many different ways:
   - The two teachers may divide the lesson, each teaching different parts.
   - One teacher may actually teach the lesson, the other taking a role which includes monitoring student behavior, scribing on the overhead or chart paper, supporting specific students, and adapting the instructions or expectations of the assignment.
   - One teacher may model a lesson for the other teacher on a current learning strategy.
   - Together, the teachers may conduct a reading or writing assessment to monitor student growth and to inform future plans for teaching.

2. The resource teacher and classroom teacher may take separate groups of students:
   - The resource teacher may take one group to work on a specific skill such as adding to ten; the classroom teacher may take a group of students working with numbers to 100.
   - The class may be working on two novels, and so each teacher takes one group of students.
   - Each teacher may take a group of students to do small group or individual assessment.
   - During the writing process, one teacher may be working with most of the class while the other meets with individual students.

One rationale for co-teaching is that when two people have planned the lesson with the group and individuals in mind, then the lesson is usually richer and the activities are adapted and modified for individual students. Both teachers then know what they are going to do and what students may need individual assistance to begin their work.

— Margaret Dixon, principal

B. Working with small groups or individual students

1. One teacher works with a select group of students while the other teaches the whole class:
   - A small group may be working on a specific project to extend their learning.
   - A small group may need some pre-teaching of vocabulary that will be introduced in the upcoming theme/unit/chapter.
   - A small group may need some work in specific skills such as decoding, study strategies, and note-taking.
2. One teacher works with a student, targeting the instruction to the goals outlined on this student's Individual Education Plan.
3. One teacher works with an individual or small group of students collecting assessment data necessary to monitor student progress and to plan further intervention.

C. Consultation

1. In many cases, the co-planning or consultation is all that is required. Often, if the classroom teacher and resource teacher work together to co-plan a unit of study, and outline ways to adapt and modify for individual students, decide on criteria, or develop assessment tools, the classroom teacher feels comfortable teaching the unit alone.
2. The resource person may conduct MAPS sessions for individual students (see Chapter 9).

D. Peer/Parent/Tutor programming

1. Many resource teachers block out periods of time to train peer and parent tutors and then include them in their program. Resource teachers who have been successful in this area find they are able to meet a wider range of student needs.

E. Special Education Assistants

1. The resource teacher helps in the development of, and monitoring of, programs for the special education assistants who give specific support to students on individual education plans.

Collaborating with the Classroom Teacher

As you will note, the menu does not indicate the location of service delivery. The location is omitted purposefully because often when teachers and resource teachers meet, the *first* item on the agenda is where the service will take place rather than what service is needed.

If the conversation focuses on the goals of the teacher and children in the classroom, rather than the location, the planning process changes dramatically. The question of whether the service will take place in the classroom or as a pullout program is really the last and least important question to be asked. If it's the first one, then the teachers would be obliged to figure out who they should pull out and why. Noncategorical resource teachers prefer to talk about what classroom teachers and their

The goals of the individual or group program are designed based on the needs of the students.

students need and then decide how the teachers can work together. They might very well choose to pull some kids out, with either the resource teacher or the classroom teacher teaching the class.

When teachers understand there are many options and begin to work with them, the decision of pullout versus in-class delivery becomes irrelevant. The *plan*, based on the discussion of needs, is the critical element.

We can remember the nightmare of having a full schedule of pullout programs and thirty referrals for new students sitting in our letter trays. As learning assistance teachers, we listened to our colleagues talk about their case loads and about the stress . . . "How will I be able to see all these kids? What am I going to do?" "I change my schedule over and over again and still I can't see all the kids."

Thirty new referrals meant that you needed to talk to teachers, observe students, assess and evaluate the students, plan programs, and somehow get some children off your case load in order to put new students on. It was the old cure mentality. We needed to cure the ones we were working with first, in order to take new children on. No wonder we worried all the time, because we managed to cure so few!

When working as a noncategorical resource teacher in the classroom, you get to know all of the children and their classroom teachers very well. You and the classroom teacher are in constant conversation about all the children, you discuss adaptations and modifications, you figure out ways to enrich the program for some students. Because you know all of the children, because you see them doing daily work, because you are in the classroom watching them struggle with writing, make inappropriate comments during carpet time, or rise to a challenge, you are doing assessment all the time. You and the classroom teacher now discuss what is happening for individual children in the classroom comfortably. Adaptations are made with much more ease because you know the context and the child. Rarely now are you asked to "assess" a child the way you used to, using a standardized battery of tests. And when you are, you are not cancelling your pullout groups to do it, but doing it during the time you would have been in the classroom.

You find that referral forms are no longer needed because you know the children and are continually problem-solving. You no longer feel like you are totally responsible for "saving" children who previously were names on a referral form. True collaboration is an incredible stress reducer as you and your colleagues share the load.

Of course, no referral forms does not imply that there is no paper work to be done. Individual Education Plans remain essential, but many resource teachers have found that the nature of the IEP changes dramatically due to the shift in service delivery. The IEP, now classroom based, is a living document that both the resource teacher and classroom teacher use *daily*.

Making the Service Delivery Menu Work

When teachers see there is a menu of choices, their thinking on how to best work with a resource person often changes. Many classroom teachers have experienced working with special education or ESL resource people in only one way — pullout programs where the resource person does something to "fix" the children. If you ask classroom teachers what they want or need, many will still respond by saying, "I'd like you to assess and work with these three or six or ten kids," because this is all they have known.

Resource teachers may wish to structure their first meeting with a classroom teacher in such a way that it takes the focus off individual students and puts it on the teacher and the class as a whole. Alternatively, the classroom teacher may be the catalyst for change by requesting a different type of service from a resource person who has traditionally offered only one way of service delivery. Classroom teachers may want to consider the questions that appear in Checklist for Assessing the Nature of Service Delivery, on the next page.

Basic prerequisites to successful collaboration are trust, flexibility, and good communication skills. For two people to work closely together, share their needs safely with each other, teach in front of each other, and make plans work, they must feel confident that what takes place in the classroom is not talked about elsewhere.

There are a variety of ways for the resource teacher to make a timetable. Some of them are outlined below. A sample timetable appears on page 85.

Build a collaborative timetable. One resource teacher we know calls together the classroom teachers she is working with. They briefly describe their needs and wishes, then all of them make up the timetable. The resource teacher leads the discussion and speaks about the varying needs in the classrooms, but lets the teachers make most of the decisions. She's found over time that, for the most part, the teachers are very responsive to others' needs. Teachers may not have their wishes met, but they understand why, are more aware of the bigger picture, and have taken part in the decision-making process.

Create flexible timetables. Many resource teachers make up flexible timetables. They put a schedule in place for a period of time such as October to December. They may spend more time with a few teachers in this period, and then switch to spending more time with a different few in January.

Prioritize needs and wishes. Some resource teachers invite the teachers that they are responsible for to give them their classroom timetables and with colored pens outline the periods they wish the resource teacher would be available to work with them. They prioritize the areas by color or number. The resource teacher then works with the timetables like a jigsaw puzzle, trying to meet as many high priority needs as possible.

Checklist for Assessing the Nature
of Service Delivery

The classroom teacher is ultimately responsible for the educational programming of the students in his or her classroom. Bearing this in mind, review the following questions.

1. Can you account for or explain what is happening to support the students' learning while they are out of the room with a specialist (teacher, counsellor . . .)?

2. Is the program that the specialist has set up in concert with the learning program of your classroom and of the designated student?

3. Were you part of the planning of the program and the decision of where service delivery takes place?

4. Have you ever questioned where service delivery is taking place?

5. Have you invited your learning assistance teacher, or your ESL teacher, or a reading teacher in the classroom to work with your students in a collaborative way?

6. Do you think there is transfer of what is being taught outside the classroom to work situations inside the classroom?

7. Are the students becoming more independent as learners as a result of your combined efforts?

Develop mini-units based on staff need. In one school, the intermediate staff said they needed to work with students on study strategies. Instead of each intermediate teacher developing the strategies, they brainstormed for the most important ideas and developed an outline together. The resource teacher then co-taught the unit with each classroom teacher, adapting and changing the unit based on all of the experiences that she was having in each classroom. At the end of the unit, the teachers had developed a mini-course that each of them could then use every year within their classrooms.

In a similar instance, a resource teacher and a classroom teacher developed a number of lessons to introduce and use during buddy reading in the classroom. The resource teacher and classroom teacher then offered to work with any teacher in the school who would also like to use the unit.

Resource teachers who do this on a regular basis generally block out a period of time each week and offer that period on a rotating basis to anyone on staff. This type of service delivery needs to be discussed and agreed to by the staff as a whole.

Holding the Resource Team Model Up to the Light

Resources teachers need to be actively involved with students and teachers in September. However, some resource teachers spend September (and even October) assessing students and doing IEPs, and then cancelling programs again in January and June to update IEPs. When resource teams choose to do this they communicate negative messages:

- that paper work is more important than working with children and teachers;
- that identification of students "to get more money" is the ultimate goal, secondary to making real changes for those students; and
- that IEP writing is something done in the back room and will, in some magical way, help the child.

Working with teachers and students to make changes for children in a visible, collaborative way, on a daily basis, is the highest priority — and needs to come first. Classroom teachers have a great deal of paper work to do especially around report card time. Resource teachers have a great deal of paper work to do throughout the year. And they do need time to talk and plan and write IEPs together. However, it is detrimental to the image of the team, and to service delivery for students, when resource teams cancel programs to do their paper work.

Often, in September, it is not possible to write up a timetable for resource teachers such as the one that appears on page 85. Class reviews have not taken place, needs have not been established, and teacher timetables are in flux. September is a great month for resource teachers

What a Day Might Look Like for a Noncategorical Resource Teacher

8:15 – 9:00   School-based team meeting

9:00 – 10:00   (A) co-teach – Grade 5/6 classroom

Reading/Writers' Workshop: Roles of both classroom teacher and resource teacher call for teaching mini-lessons, conferencing with students about their reading/writing projects, assisting with materials, developing criteria, and doing assessment.

10:00 – 10:30   (B) works with large group while teacher works with small group — Grade 2/3 classroom.

Individual Reading: Resource teacher confers with individual students about their reading and keeps notes for the classroom teacher. Classroom teacher works with a select group of students on specific reading skills and strategies.

10:45 – 12:00   (A) co-teach — Grade 1/2 classroom

Reading/Writing: Resource teacher models reading/writing strategies that the classroom teacher would like to learn. Both teachers work with students during student response.

12:25 – 1:00   co-plans with the Grade 1/2 teacher

1:00 – 1:30   (B) works with small group while teacher works with large group — Grade 1/2 classroom.

Individual Reading: "Book Time." Classroom teacher confers with individual students; resource teacher works with the same two Grade 2 children each day to teach skills and strategies (letter recognition/sounds/common words/fluency).

1:30 – 2:15   (A) co-teaching with all primary teachers

Primary Math Centres: All primary teachers and resource teacher work with small groups during this time, rotating through all of the groups.

2:15 – 3:00   (B) works with large group while teacher works with small group — Grade 4/5 classroom.

Individual Reading: Resource teacher works with most of the class doing independent reading; the classroom teacher takes a small group to work on specific reading skills and strategies.

to be in classrooms getting to know teachers and their new students. During this time there are many options for them, including these:

- observing individual students that you had concerns about last year;
- assisting in the transition for some students moving from one teacher to another;
- modifying behavior programs for students so that the transition is more easily made;
- working closely with classroom teachers who are receiving students who need major adaptations or modifications so that the teacher can assist the student from the start;
- modelling strategies that worked for particular students; and
- teaching the whole class while the teacher gets to know students individually.

More permanent schedules can begin to form after class reviews have taken place and the resource teachers have been in the classes working with and getting to know students, and listening to teachers' needs.

Reflecting on the Value of the Noncategorical Resource Teacher Model

When staff in a school "walk the talk" of collaboration, a model is set for students. Students no longer see an "expert" model where students are whisked down the hall for "special" programs. Rather they see ongoing decision making and problem solving as professionals employ the best of their practice to create positive learning environments for all students. Students see teachers reflecting alone and together on their practice. They learn to respect differences and to employ the social aspects of learning. Since labeling and pullout programs are less common, students are not set up by their differences or the places where they receive their programming. Belonging in the classroom increases their feelings of security and hence, the ability to learn.

Implementing Class Reviews

8

"You can't be a team member without being a part of the conversation. You'd just become a technician without reflection, and teaching just has to be so much more than that."

— Steve Rosell, teacher

School-based teams play a crucial role in developing safe and inclusive schools. They make so many decisions about children's lives, and their language influences teachers, parents, and students. If school-based teams have tunnel vision, speak categorically, or use judgmental language, then everyone in the school is affected in subtle or nonsubtle ways.

Many school-based teams set in place processes for dealing with issues, whether they are whole-school, classroom, or individual issues. Some of these processes work better than others in promoting open communication, collaboration, and a real and optimistic sense of problem solving.

Most school-based teams include people in the following roles: school administrator(s), school-based resource teachers, school counsellor, school nurse, and classroom teacher of the student or class to be discussed. Some teams also include the school librarian.

These school-based teams invite other personnel to attend meetings if they are involved with a given classroom or child: these include school-based special education assistants, child-care workers, and district personnel such as the speech and language pathologist, and teachers of the hearing or visually impaired.

Making changes to how school-based teams operate is sometimes very difficult. Some teams become overly concerned with labelling and diagnosing and forget that the real job is to look closely at a child and do some sensitive and sincere problem solving that will help the child today.

Teams who are committed to inclusion develop strategies and processes that keep individual children the focus. They work hard to support the classroom teacher in meeting the needs of individual children and the class as a whole. Team members spend much less time on paper work, and much more time problem solving and teaching. The structure of meetings that school-based teams hold can influence staff perceptions about inclusion. "Class Reviews" are one example.

The Changing Nature of Class Reviews

Traditionally, class reviews have focused on sharing the needs of individual students in each classroom. In many schools, the school-based team sits down with each classroom teacher in September or October and the group reviews the class together. Often the classroom teacher will go through the class list, and the teacher and team members will share information about each child: learning needs, social or emotional needs, medical history, speech and language, and so on. At the end of the meeting, the resource teacher, nurse, counsellor, and administrator, as well as the classroom teacher, all have lists of students to see or things to do. In most cases, everyone leaves feeling overwhelmed after focusing only on the things that need doing, and the students who have specific needs.

Some teams design these meetings to be descriptive of not only individual students but the context of the classroom where these students spend their day. The meetings are more positive, encompass a wider range of topics, and allow the team members more insight into how they might work in meaningful ways with the classroom teacher. The classroom teacher is asked to paint a picture of the class by describing the strengths and needs of the class as a whole and to outline personal goals for the year. Then all team members share information about individual students. Student strengths and needs are seen in the context of the classroom rather than in isolation.

Preparing for the Meeting

Class reviews usually take about 45 to 60 minutes a classroom. Usually teachers-on-call are asked to take over classrooms on a rotating basis throughout one or two days. Before the meeting it is advisable for classroom teachers to mull over the following questions.

A Framework for Class Review:
The Classroom Teacher's Perspective

1. What are the strengths of the class? What are the positive things about this group as a whole?

2. What are your concerns about the class as a whole? What do you wonder about?

3. What are your main goals this year?
   (These goals may be based on the strengths and/or concerns, or on an area of interest, or a new grade level or new curriculum. Each teacher may have three or four.)

4. What are the individual needs in your classroom? (medical, learning, social-emotional, language, or other concerns related to individual students)

A Class Review That Models Inclusion

Each 45 to 60 minute meeting needs a facilitator and a recorder. An example of a recording form, which can be enlarged to fit an 11" x 17" (279 mm x 432 mm) page, appears on the next page.

In the scenario below, the school-based team includes the classroom teacher, the special education assistant who spends most of her day in that teacher's classroom, the counsellor, the nurse, two resource teachers, and the principal. Team members meet together at an appointed time, with refreshments set up in the room. The meeting begins after everyone is comfortable. One of the resource teachers serves as facilitator.

Facilitator (to the classroom teacher): I want to explain a little about the process that we will be using today in the class review. We are going to begin by looking at the strengths of your class as a whole, then the needs of the class as a whole, and your specific goals for the year or term. The reason we do this is because we think it's really important to look at the strengths and needs of the students in the context of the *whole* classroom. After we finish that part, we will all share information about specific students. You'll share information you have with us, and different people on the team will share information with you. This is *not* a time for IEP planning. You and your resource teacher need to choose a half day next week to plan. Okay? Please describe the strengths of your class.

Establishing Classroom Strengths

Teacher: Hmm, well, they are really a very caring group of kids. They treat each other nicely, they cooperate, they love to work together as buddies or in small groups. They're good listeners, and follow directions pretty well. Would you agree, Deb?

Teaching Assistant: Yes, there's a real solid group of kids who go out of their way to help other kids, or encourage them somehow. It's neat to see.

Throughout the review, the recorder records information, clarifying if necessary.

Facilitator: Sounds like a great group of kids. You've talked about them socially, and how they follow directions. How are they doing academically?

Teacher: Academically, they seem on top of things. There are some kids I'm concerned about, but quite a few are very strong and most of the others seem like they're where they should be. It's hard to tell for sure yet. As a class they love stories and they love art — painting, drawing, anything they can create with their hands.

Resource Teacher 2: Isn't there also a core that love Phys. Ed. and any other physical play?

Classroom Strengths

- caring group of kids
- treat each other nicely
- cooperative
- love to work together (buddies/small groups)
- good listeners
- follow directions well
- help and encourage others
- academically okay
- love stories, art, creating with their hands
- enjoy gym and outside play

Class Review Recording Form

Classroom Needs

Classroom Strengths

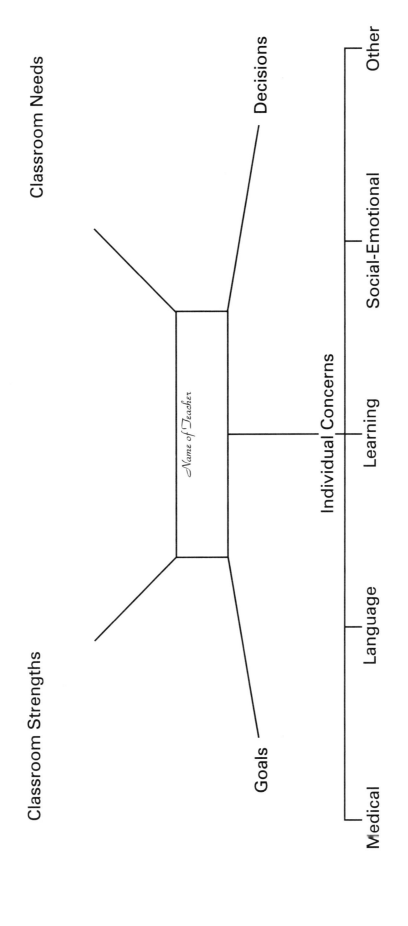

Name of Teacher

Decisions

Goals

Individual Concerns

Medical | Language | Learning | Social-Emotional | Other

Teacher: Oh yes! We've got a whole group that would spend all day in the gym or outside.

Facilitator: Thanks. That creates a good picture. You have a lot of strengths there. If you think of any other strengths, just say them and we can record them later. Let's move to class concerns. Do you have any concerns in terms of the whole class, things that you wonder about?

Expressing General Concerns

Classroom Concerns

- kids' inability to problem-solve on their own
- exclusion of some students; 4 or 5 students set the tone
- parental commitment to learning or follow-through is questionable

Teacher: Yes, I have a few. Although the class seems to be a very caring group, they don't seem to know how to solve problems. Any incident, no matter how small, is reported to Deb or myself. I haven't found a child in the class who stands up and says, "I need you to stop doing that." Instead, all of them come seeking adult assistance. That's one area we're working on. Then there is exclusion. There are about five strong personalities in the class. They're super kids and have incredible potential to be great leaders in the school. However, they can also really affect the climate of the class. If one of them is upset with someone, you can count on five more kids ignoring or excluding the child in some way. I haven't got a handle on it yet.

Facilitator: Any other concerns?

Teacher: Parental involvement. Again, I have a nice group — they come in and chat — but I'm unsure about their commitment to helping their children really learn. Follow-through on things seems to be quite a problem. I've been wondering if I should hold some evening meetings, or send home more newsletters, or figure out ways to get them into the classroom. I sometimes get the feeling there is a hidden agenda, or a misunderstanding of what our class needs, but I'm not sure. Some unrest or something. I need to figure out a plan. I've already talked with Janet and Leah (the principal) about the matter and we've been throwing around some ideas.

Facilitator: Okay, let's put working with parents under the goals section, seeing as you are already making some plans there. Anything else?

Teacher: No, I don't think so. Those are the major things right now.

Determining Goals

Goals

- working with parents
- class meetings
- increased communication between teacher and teaching assistant
- writing process
- math centres
- friendship circles

Facilitator: Let's look at goals now. When you think about both the strengths and needs of your class, plus your own goals in teaching this year, what do you see as your main foci?

Teacher: Well, besides the parent meetings or information, I want to work on classroom meetings. It's not something I've done before. It may be a way to get at some of the problem-solving issues. I'd love anything you have that I might read.

Also, Debbie and I are working on figuring out ways to communicate more efficiently. We might start a book, or find a way to meet briefly at least once a day.

I want to focus on the writing process too this year and figure out ways to encourage every child to write and feel successful. And I'm working on setting up individual math centres in my classroom to reinforce what I'm teaching in different math areas. I've already started that by compiling all this stuff.

Debbie, do you want to talk about what we were saying about friendship circles?

Teaching Assistant: Yes, we're looking at finding ways to make a friendship circle of some kind for both Jamie and Jessica. We want it to be real, not artificial, so we're looking at who would be potential friends for both of these rather isolated kids. I'm really keen on this because I've done some reading and I've got time at recess and lunch to promote the idea — if we can just figure out ways to do it.

Facilitator: Sounds like a lot of new things! Let's consider how the resource team could help you in any of those areas.

Teacher: Well, I don't know. Like give me materials?

Counsellor: I have lots of background in class meetings. Maybe there's a way I could fit in, and we could focus on some of those social concerns. I've also got some material on friendship circles, and I know some people who are using them in other schools that you might want to talk to.

Teaching Assistant: I'd love to see the materials. Thanks.

Resource Teacher: When we meet for planning next week, maybe we could talk about how I might team with you in writing or math as part of our time together.

Facilitator: Think about it, because there are several possibilities there.

Teacher: I will for sure. Thanks.

Facilitator: Okay, under decisions, let's put Sheri (the counsellor) to give Deb materials on friendship circles, and should we note that you'll talk with Sheri and Janet (the resource teacher) about class meetings, math centres, and the writing process?

Teacher: For sure.

Identifying Individual Students' Needs

Facilitator: Thanks, Donna. Now let's move to the section called individual concerns. We'll start with medical concerns and Nadia (the nurse) can fill us in. If anyone else has information, please let us know.

Nurse: There are only three kids I know about. Sonny gets bad headaches and occasionally needs to be sent home, but I think it only occurred a couple of times last year. Kinder has asthma. Again, it's not severe but you should keep an eye on her when she's in Phys. Ed. and be sure she has her inhaler when you go on field trips.

Teacher: Yes, her mom mentioned it. I guess it got pretty bad this summer for awhile but seems to have calmed down again.

Nurse: I'll note that. Okay, then there's Jamie. Jamie, you all know, has lots of medical history but is doing amazingly well. He is not toilet-trained and the doctors say he may never be, but he may surprise us yet — on occasion, he does go to the bathroom. Isn't that right, Donna?

Teacher: Yes. It's quite exciting. I kind of think he's starting to take the cues and once he does that you never know!

Nurse: That's great. Jamie has lots of other medical problems such as heart murmur, but toileting is the major one at school. We just have to keep an eye on him when he's very physical, but he seems to cope pretty well. Deb and Donna have a good grasp on what to watch for.

Facilitator: Any other concerns? No? Okay, let's move to language issues.

Student Language Needs

- Timmy, Quan, Shuster — ESL (Level 1)

Teacher: There are three kids in the class who are new Canadians and have very limited English. All of them are at level 1 on the ESL assessments. They are Timmy, Quan and Shuster. Timmy and Quan are fitting in really well and already have kids to play with. Shuster is the only one I'm concerned about. He is really impulsive. He sits very restlessly on the carpet, he throws blocks off the table, he pushes kids — all with a smile on his face. He talks a blue streak, but it's all mumbled and kind of strange. For example, if you talk to him about throwing stuff he begins to talk about a dog, or chasing someone on the playground. I've tried talking to his mom but she has limited English too. I wrote everything out for her because she said she'd get it interpreted, but the next day I found my note in Shuster's book used as a book mark. I don't really know what to do next.

Recorder: I've put Shuster under language concerns, but it sounds like he also fits under social-emotional.

Teacher: That's for sure.

Principal: It sounds like we need to find an interpreter. Let's figure that out after the meeting, and I'll contact one and get a meeting set up with mom and dad.

Teacher: I don't think there is a dad. But a meeting would be great. Thanks.

Facilitator: Let's move to learning.

Learning Needs

- Shane, Elizabeth, Narra, Jamie — language arts, math, fine motor skills
- Jessica, Tom — expressing ideas
- Ruth — writing prolifically
- Paul — challenge in math
- Justin — challenge in all areas

Teacher: I've listed the kids in a couple of ways. Three of them have a lot of needs overall — language arts and math, fine motor, etc. They are Shane, Elizabeth, and Narra. Jamie could fit there too. And then there's Jessica and Tom who need lots of help in expressing their ideas. Really, there are more than that but those are the two along with the other four I mentioned that I'm most concerned about.

Then I'm also concerned about keeping a few others stimulated enough — Ruth, Justin, and Paul. Paul is already doing math about five years ahead of his age! Ruth is a prolific writer and Justin does everything well beyond expectations — he's thorough, thoughtful, organized, and just works away quietly.

The rest of the class is okay, I think. Verbally there is a whole crew who need encouragement, but that will come with time.

Facilitator: What about the social-emotional area?

Teacher: Well, I've mentioned Shuster. He's having difficulty settling in, but the kids are really quite patient with him. I am more worried about Jamie who, at this point, is very isolated, as is Jessica. Jessica is new, hardly speaks at all, and when she does, she whispers. But she has another side to her. She is shy but she's also sneaky, I think. I see her do things like write on kids' work when they aren't looking, sneak a pencil from someone's desk, tear a book, etc. The kids don't particularly like her, and I know a group of girls ostracize her and get all the kids to stay away. I am upset about this little group of girls — but I'm also worried about them because obviously they feel they need to show they are better than she is. Instead of helping her, they make things worse.

Facilitator: Some of these issues you plan to work through with class meetings and friendship circles?

Teacher: Right.

Facilitator: Okay. Thanks. It looks like you've got a good grasp on things already. Did you want to add anything more to any of the sections?

Teacher: No, I thing that's fine. How about you, Deb?

Teaching Assistant. No.

Facilitator: Okay. Let's review the decisions. Then before we leave let's review dates for follow-up. You're meeting next week on Jamie? And would you like to set a date for Jessica as well?

Teacher: Yes.

The school-based team reviews decisions and sets dates for IEP meetings, and then sub-groups set up times to talk about and plan re: the writing process, math centres, and friendship circles.

The next page shows a completed form based on the class review just presented. It is an accurate reflection of a review where the school-based team and the classroom teacher took an inclusive view of the strengths and needs of the whole class.

Using such a form does not mean the focus of the conversation will change. Some team leaders use these forms, go quickly through the strengths, concerns, and goals, and then focus most of the time on individual needs. They then draw all the decisions from the individual needs section. In other words, to change the focus from individual students to the teacher and whole class, you need to believe that working with the teacher to meet her or his needs is one way of making real differences for children, one way of meeting their needs.

The process for a class review based on inclusive values does not automatically change attitudes. It is only one way to assist staff if the attitudes and beliefs are already there, or one way to influence attitudes if some of the team members believe in it.

Student Social-Emotional Needs

- Shuster — difficulty settling in
- Jamie — isolated/no friends
- Jessica — isolated/whispers/no friends
- group of girls who ostracize Jessica

Sample Class Review Web

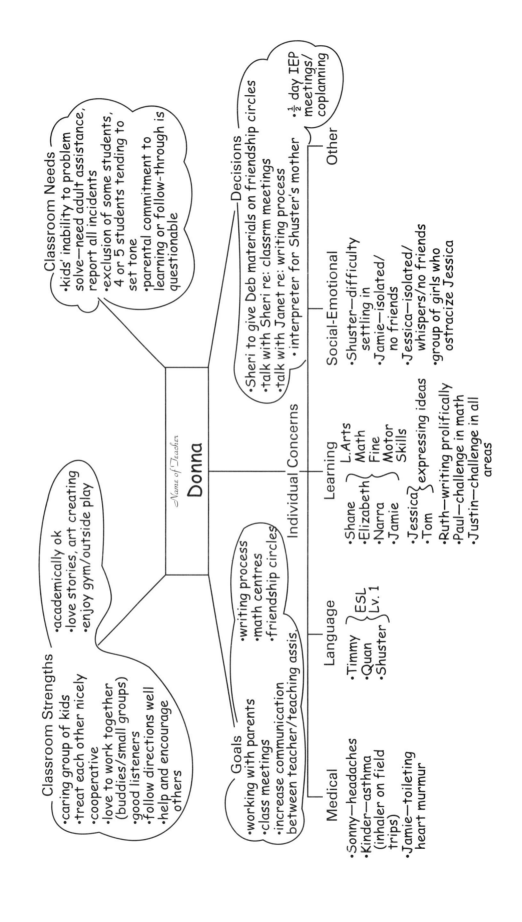

Classroom Strengths
- academically ok
- love stories, art creating
- enjoy gym/outside play
- caring group of kids
- treat each other nicely
- cooperative
- love to work together (buddies/small groups)
- good listeners
- follow directions well
- help and encourage others

Classroom Needs
- kids' inability to problem solve—need adult assistance, report all incidents
- exclusion of some students, 4 or 5 students tending to set tone
- parental commitment to learning or follow-through is questionable

Name of Teacher
Donna

Goals
- writing process
- math centres
- friendship circles
- working with parents
- class meetings
- increase communication between teacher/teaching assis

Decisions
- Sheri to give Deb materials on friendship circles
- talk with Sheri re: classrm meetings
- talk with Janet re: writing process
- interpreter for Shuster's mother

Other
- ½ day IEP meetings/ coplanning

Individual Concerns

Medical
- Sonny—headaches
- Kinder—asthma (inhaler on field trips)
- Jamie—toileting heart murmur

Language
- Timmy
- Quan   } ESL Lv. 1
- Shuster

Learning
- Shane
- Elizabeth
- Narra
- Jamie   } L.Arts Math Fine Motor Skills
- Jessica
- Tom   } expressing ideas
- Ruth—writing prolifically
- Paul—challenge in math
- Justin—challenge in all areas

Social-Emotional
- Shuster—difficulty settling in
- Jamie—isolated/ no friends
- Jessica—isolated/ whispers/no friends group of girls who ostracize Jessica

9

MAPS: Planning for Individual Students

"The concept of difference should not be scary. Clearly people are different. The concept of difference is only scary when put into a hierarchy."

— David Hingsburger, educational consultant

Planning for some students is more complex that it is for others. Either the teacher or the parent is not satisfied with what is happening for the student in the classroom. It thus becomes necessary to align parent and school goals. To accomplish this, some schools pull together the key people in the student's life to set reasonable and consistent goals and plan a cohesive program, understood by each person who deals with the child. Such a problem-solving session happens because the child, teacher, or parents need a more in-depth planning process. Regardless of who initiates the process, the child's needs remain paramount through it.

A planning model called MAPS (Multi Action Planning System) was developed by Marsha Forest and Judith Snow at McGill University. It came about when educators decided it would be a good idea to include students who had attended special classes elsewhere in regular classes at neighborhood schools. Facilitators for MAPS were trained all over Canada. MAPS was initially developed for students who were intellectually challenged or had multiple handicaps. It was a way of looking at the whole child in their whole life — classroom, school, home, and community. The process was designed to include parents as partners in their child's education.

Teachers began to see the incredible benefit of looking at students in this way, of receiving input from many people in the child's life, and in developing in-depth and consistent plans. Modifications of this process sprang up in many schools. Shorter and less in-depth sessions were used with students whose needs were less complex but who could benefit from consistent planning. In fact, many teachers have told us that they wish they had the time to use such a process with all of the students in the school.

The focused conversation of a MAPS session helps all participants become not just informed, but enabled, to work more productively, as a team, with a student.

MAPS is a collaborative problem-solving process. It helps develop a feeling of working together to meet a student's needs. The process relies on everyone's input in terms of who the student is and what he is able to do. Teachers, parents, and students, through participation in the process, tend to put aside any disagreements and focus on a mutually agreed-upon plan.

Focusing on One Student

1. Who will attend the meeting?

Anyone who could add some information that would help make a meaningful and successful plan should come. The school personnel, along with the parents and student, decide who should attend. Each key person has a different relationship with the student, knows the student in a different way, and therefore will see the student differently. All key people will have different views on what works with this student. These divergent ideas are what makes the meeting rich and meaningful.

2. Who will facilitate?

It is best if the facilitator is an "outside person," in the sense that they may not know the student very well, and have no personal agenda or preconceived ideas on what the outcomes of the meeting should be.

The facilitator does not participate in the content of the meeting. Instead, this person ensures that the meeting follows a process, everyone has a chance to talk, no one dominates, ideas are recorded clearly and concisely, the time frame is respected, and a plan is made or at least begun by the end of the meeting. The facilitator needs to be adept at clarifying and clustering the ideas put forward, listening carefully and respectfully to each individual, and encouraging ideas from each person.

3. What needs to happen before the meeting?

Set a time: A meeting time that is agreeable to all needs to be determined. Usually these meetings occur after school or, if teachers can be released, they can be scheduled during the school day. In order to reach a plan, 1-1/2 hours is the *minimum* that should be scheduled.

Focus your thinking: Each invitee should receive a copy of the following questions to review.

> What are your dreams for _____?
> What are your concerns/nightmares?
> What are his/her strengths?
> What are his/her needs?

If a person cannot attend she might give input on paper to someone who will be present.

Sometimes the student is asked these questions:

What are your dreams for yourself?
What are your concerns?
What are your strengths? or What are you really good at?
What are your needs? or What do you think you need to work on?

If the student cannot write responses himself, then someone who is detached from the answers that the student gives can scribe for him or assist him in some way.

The questions are intended to stimulate thinking only, to provide a focus for the conversation. They do not need to be filled out or brought to the meeting. Answers are never collected. Individuals will share what they want to share during the meeting itself. In some cases the student or a parent decides that it's best if the student is not in attendance.

4. How should the meeting be set up?

Ideally, the meeting will take place in a warm, comfortable room where chairs can be gathered in a circle and where everyone can see each other.

The facilitator will need to make up four charts, one for each question, provide some colored pens, and find a place to put up each of the charts after they are completed so that all of the group can refer back to them.

5. How should the meeting unfold?

Begin with a welcome and a review of the objectives and roles. Next, gather and record information on the charts about dreams, concerns, strengths, and needs. Follow this discussion with a short break, then set priorities for planning based on the information gathered on the charts. Finally, begin to make a plan.

A Model MAPS Meeting

M   Multi
A   Action
P   Planning
S   System

Kevin is a Grade 5 student. Kevin's classroom teacher feels Kevin is being challenged by the work he is given in school, but Kevin's parents do not. They would like to see some changes in Kevin's program, and would like some input on how it's done. Kevin's teacher and the parents have met many times and have been unable to resolve the issue to the parents' satisfaction.

Step 1: Welcome/Objectives/Roles

Facilitator: I'd like to thank all of you for coming to spend some time talking about Kevin and his program here at school. Before we start the meeting, I want to be sure that everyone here knows who everyone else is. Let's take a minute to go around the table and have each person say their name and explain their relationship with Kevin.

Kevin, a friend of Kevin's, the classroom teacher, the parents, a resource teacher, the principal, and the facilitator introduce each other.

Facilitator: Thank you. I'm Jesse, and I also work as a resource teacher in the school, but not with Kevin's classroom.

Today, we are going to be working together for about one and a half hours. During that time we will be using a planning process to look at Kevin's strengths and needs, what is currently happening for Kevin in school, and what everyone would like to see happen for Kevin. This process depends on everyone sharing their dreams and concerns for Kevin, and then looking at his strengths and needs. By the end of the meeting, we will begin to make a plan together.

Kevin, I want to encourage you to speak up as much as possible, even though it might be difficult to talk in front of everyone. It is really important for all of us to know what you think about each of the questions that I ask.

The facilitator explains his role is to ask the questions, record the information, and move the group toward a plan. He will seek to clarify the others' thinking.

Facilitator: We are going to work through the four questions I gave you to think about. Then we will have a short break, prioritize the areas we want to look at, and begin to make a plan.

Step 2: Gather and record information on the charts about dreams, concerns, strengths, and needs.

Facilitator: We are going to begin by looking at dreams: the dreams you have for yourself, Kevin, and the dreams that your mom and dad, and your teachers have for you. These dreams might be for this year in Grade 5. They may be for your high school years or for you as an adult. Because we want to be sure we hear everyone's dreams for Kevin, we'll start by going around the circle. If you want to pass, just ask us to come back to you.

Kevin, would you feel comfortable starting? What is a dream you have for yourself?

Kevin: I'd like to become a paleontologist after I graduate.

The facilitator begins recording information on the appropriate chart. This activity continues throughout the meeting.

Facilitator: Really, you said two dreams there: one to become a paleontologist, and the other, to graduate. Is that right?

Kevin: Yes, I guess so.

Facilitator: Are you thinking you'd be a paleontologist after graduating from high school or university?

Kevin: Well, I was thinking high school, but I also think I'd like to go to university some day, too.

Facilitator: Okay. (to Kevin's mother) Ann, what is one of your dreams for Kevin?

Mother: I'd like to see Kevin challenged this year in school, and all through the rest of elementary and high school.

Facilitator: Are there any specific areas you're thinking about?

Mother: Mostly in math, but also in writing.

The facilitator next invites Kevin's teacher to speak.

Teacher: My dream for Kevin is that he graduates from university, has a successful career, and maintains the same attitude that he has now of caring for others, and being willing to assist others who don't do as well as he does. Basically, that he continues to be such a kind and caring individual.

The facilitator summarizes these ideas as best she can.

Facilitator: Does that sum up what you were saying or was there more?

Teacher: No, that's fine.

The facilitator continues to gather and record information, often asking for clarification to be sure what is being recorded is really what the person is meaning. If only one area of the child's development is being talked about, the facilitator may probe. For example: "We have quite a few dreams for Kevin about his future in terms of education and his career. Does anyone have other dreams for Kevin, for example, about his emotional or social life, family, friends?"

After going around the circle two or three times and recording a wide range of ideas, the facilitator concludes the dreams area.

Facilitator: I see a lot of dreams here for you, Kevin. Do you have any others you'd like to add before we move on? Or does anyone else have another one?

The participants indicate that they are satisfied with the list.

Facilitator: We'll put the dream chart over here for now. If at any time during the meeting you'd like to add to it, please do so.

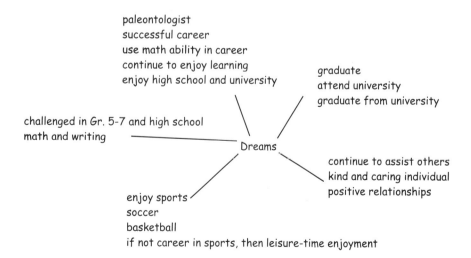

Facilitator: We're now going to look at any concerns we have for Kevin. These concerns may be things we are afraid might get in the way of his reaching the dreams that we've talked about. Again, Kevin, if you don't mind, we'll start with you.

Kevin: Well, I've thought about this one a lot since you gave me the questions. I couldn't really think of any concerns, but now that we've talked about my dreams, I guess I worry that my eyesight will get worse and I won't be able to get a good job or drive.

Facilitator: Thanks, Kevin. I can see that could really be a concern.

The facilitator begins recording information on concerns.

Facilitator: Ann, we'll move on to you.

Mother: I'm concerned that Kevin might lose interest in school if he's bored, and then won't complete school and go to university. I want so badly for him to stay motivated, be keen to try new things, and not feel he's just doing things over and over. I'm afraid if he has to do multiplication questions again he's just going to give up and say, "To heck with it, I'm bored."

Facilitator: So, there are a number of concerns there: one, that he'll be bored, then not complete high school and university, and two, that he'll give up. I also heard that you're concerned that he's repeating too many things at school, things that he already knows, such as multiplication. Is that right?

Mother: That is exactly right.

The facilitator turns to the classroom teacher.

Teacher: My concerns are similar to Ann's. I love to watch Kevin learn because he's keen, but I too am afraid that he might get discouraged. I guess my concern is that, because Kevin is such a nice guy, he won't tell me when he already knows something, when something is boring or redundant to him. I can't always know.

Facilitator: So you're concerned that Kevin will just continue to do something like multiplication even when he knows he doesn't need any more practice. Why?

Teacher: Oh, because he doesn't want to be a bother maybe. Or maybe he doesn't understand that teachers need to know that information, that most teachers, if approached politely, would be willing to listen to him.

Facilitator: Okay. Do my notes sum it up?

Teacher: Yes.

As with the dreams, the facilitator continues to go around the circle, clarifying and probing for information. After a wide range of ideas are gathered, the facilitator again brings this focus to a close.

Facilitator: There have been some concerns voiced about Kevin's academic program, his future, his eyesight, and his motivation and assertiveness to be sure he's challenged. Does anyone have any other concerns to express before we move on?

No one offers any more so this chart is put up beside the dreams.

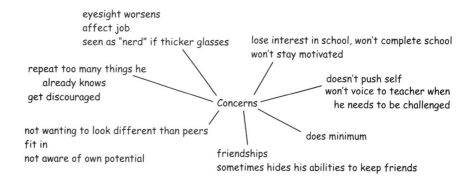

The strengths area is then addressed in a similar fashion and then the needs area.

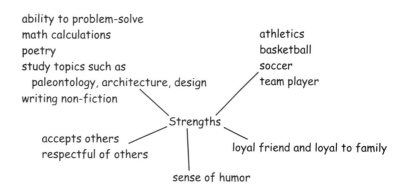

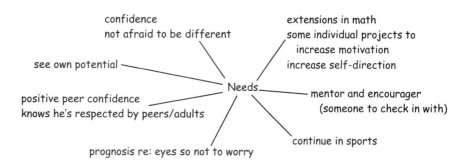

Facilitator: Before taking a short break, I'd like you to take a look at the four charts up on the wall. We have gathered a lot of information about Kevin, and I see some categories emerging: academic challenges, confidence, and medical. Do you see any others?

Father: I think those are the main ones.

Facilitator: Okay. If you see any other connections during the break, please let me know. Also, during the next ten minutes, think about priorities. Which of these areas do you think is the most important to address first?

Everyone takes a ten-minute break while the facilitator looks over the charts and formulates a plan for the next section.

Step 3: Set priorities for planning based on the information gathered on the charts.

Facilitator: Are there any other areas that you thought of?

Mother: I think those three cover them.

Facilitator: Then let's look at what our priorities are for Kevin. Does anyone feel strongly about any one or two areas?

Teacher: The area of challenging Kevin in his academic work is the one that I think is the most important to tackle first. Kevin and his parents seem very concerned about that. I certainly want to do a good job in meeting Kevin's needs, and before we leave I'd love to be able to say we had at least the beginnings of a plan.

Facilitator: Do others of you think beginning on academics is the priority? Kevin, what do you think?

Kevin: Yes, I think that's the most important, though I'm interested in learning how to be more confident. Could we look at both?

Mother: I'd like to begin with challenging Kevin and then move to confidence. I also think the medical part is important and I'm wondering if that one could be dealt with by working with our family doctor.

Others nod in agreement. The facilitator writes the three areas on the chart paper called Plan.

Step 4: The group begins to make a plan.

Facilitator: Okay, let's begin by developing a plan to ensure that Kevin's program is challenging. Then, if there's time, we'll move to confidence. In fact, these two areas may tie in nicely together. Your mom can deal with the medical aspects. Does that sound okay, Kevin?

Kevin: Yep.

Facilitator: Who would like to begin?

Resource teacher: It looks like the two subject areas that Kevin and his parents and teacher are concerned about are math and language arts. As far as math goes, we could give Kevin the chapter tests and if he gets an agreed-on percentage on certain chapters, he could skip those. We could use both the Grade 5 book and the Grade 6 book, if everyone is agreeable to acceleration in math.

Teacher: I'm fine about acceleration in math. Kevin could use Grade 5, 6, and 7 books and complete them all this year and next if he can. We could easily use the chapter tests and say if he got 85 percent correct, he could move on. There are a few problems though. The texts don't cover all of the curriculum, especially problem solving, reflection, and the use of mathematical language. He would miss the learning that comes from group interactions in math. And since we do not use all the chapters in the text, we would have to look carefully at the texts and

Plan for Kevin

Re Math:
- ✓ Do work in class.
- ✓ Same topic areas as class is working on, but with extended materials (from Grades 5-7).
- ✓ Talk with Grades 6 and 7 teachers.
- ✓ Keep records of all areas completed.

Re Research:
- ✓ Librarian will be mentor.
- ✓ Do research assignments (projects) with a small group of students in classroom (possibly three other students).
- ✓ Spend about three times a week on project. Some individual time on weekends, evenings.
- ✓ Parents will be involved in supporting/encouraging/extending individual work (public library, linking with experts in the community).

the areas he'd be missing in curriculum. Maybe I could meet with Grade 6 and 7 teachers to map out a plan. What do you think of that, Kevin?

Kevin: Well, I'd like to do harder math, but does that mean I'd have to leave the room to do math with the other grades?

Facilitator: Does that concern you?

Kevin: Yeah. I don't want to leave. I don't mind doing other work, but I don't want to make a big deal out of it.

Facilitator: What are you saying? That you don't want the other kids to notice, that you're uncomfortable going to other classes, or what?

Kevin: Well, I'm not sure. I guess I like being in my own class and I like doing math with my friends. I do like the idea of doing harder math 'cause I know I can do it, but I don't really want to sit there doing it all on my own.

Facilitator: So, if we can figure out a way to give you more difficult math concepts or applications in your own classroom, perhaps on the same topic that everyone else is doing or something similar, would that suit you?

Kevin: Yes.

Teacher: Well, maybe with extension materials, Kevin could first do all the chapters that are similar to the ones we're doing. For example: we're working on geometry now, so if Kevin gets 85 percent on the Grade 5 geometry section, then he could pull out alternative texts and use parallel, but more challenging geometry chapters. At the end of the year he will have acquired some of the concepts normally taught in Grades 6 and 7.

Principal: As long as we talk with the Grade 6 and 7 teachers about this, that might be okay. However, we'd need to keep a record of exactly what has been completed. I'm wondering if there are parts of the curriculum that are already challenging enough for Kevin or that would need only slight adaptation.

Dad: All this is okay, as long as we are talking about a plan for Grades 5, 6, and 7 and not just from now until the end of June. Everyone would have to agree because if Kevin has to repeat chapters in the same Grade 6 textbook next year, he will be more bored than ever.

Resource teacher: You're right. We'll need to talk with the teacher next year in September, but I doubt there would be a problem as we have several other students in the upper grades on accelerated programs.

The discussion continues and a plan is made for math and language arts with Kevin having to take more personal responsibility for speaking up and letting the classroom teacher and his parents know how things are going.

Step 5: Set up a follow-up meeting.

A one-hour, follow-up meeting is scheduled for one month away, to discuss confidence and medical concerns, and to get an update on how the math and research projects are going.

Reflections on MAPS

These planning sessions are time consuming, but generally very rewarding. Many teachers leave these meetings saying, "I wish there was time to have a meeting like this for all of my students." Parents feel heard and students benefit by having a program more closely designed for them. Since all of the major players are in attendance, more support and understanding between home and school can be generated.

These planning meetings can also be used to look at such issues as school-wide behavior, inclusion, clubs and teams. Furthermore, staffs, classrooms, student councils, and parent advisory groups can use the process to help set goals and plan or determine staff development needs. The MAPS session is a process that respects and includes all of those involved, helping a group of individuals work together to address concerns, make a plan, and take action.

Appendix 1: People Search Strategy

Adapted from Bellanca and Fogarty (1986), *Catch Them Thinking*

People Search is a great strategy to get students talking and sharing their knowledge with each other. It is also a good way to review material before a test, or find out how much students know on a new topic of study. It promotes active listening and develops skills in clarification and paraphrasing.

1. Create a page with four to six boxes on it. At the top write the words "Find someone who . . ." and write four to six ideas in the boxes. For example: "can *describe* what it feels like to be included," "can *tell* you about a time they helped someone," "can *imagine* what it would be like if everyone felt they belonged," "can *explain* why our school has a code of conduct," "can *list* four things they did this week to make someone else feel good," "can *name* at least one person in the school they can go to for help." (Note the words in italics that help to promote different kinds of critical thinking skills — be sure that all the students will be able to answer at least one or two of the questions.)

2. Explain to the students what a people search is all about. Show them the sheet and tell them that they will be moving around the classroom finding different individuals who can answer each question. (They must have a different person for each question.)

   • Tell the students that the people they talk to must be able to explain the answer in such a way that they are able to retell it (active listening).
   • Direct them to write down the answer or key words, or an illustration to help remember the answer given. They should say the answer back to the person and have them sign their sheets when they are sure they understand.

3. Instruct the students to circulate and ask if they can help other students once their sheets are filled in.

4. When all of the students have completed their sheets, meet as a group and debrief the answers. You might want to make a master sheet and record some of the variety of answers.

Appendix 2: Think of a Time Strategy

Used with permission of the authors, Brownlie, Close, and Wingren, *Tomorrow's Classroom Today*.

1. Students are grouped in threes.

2. Students are instructed to "think of a time when . . . " around a topic and share their thinking with their small group.

3. The first "think of a time" is as a participant — when something happened to you or you were the actor.

4. After the small-group exchange and the class sharing, one student moves to join a new group.

5. The second "think of a time" is as a witness — when you saw something.

6. After the small-group exchange and the class sharing, the second student from each group moves to find a new group.

7. The third "think of a time" is as a causal agent — when you planned or caused something to happen.

8. Again, after exchanging views in the small group and in the large one, students return to their original triad.

9. The teacher helps isolate the critical learning variables that have been shared.

10. Students reflect on the process in their triads.

11. Students reflect personally.

Appendix 3: Forms for Curriculum Adaptations

(See pages 110 and 111.)

PROGRAM ANALYSIS WORKSHEET

©Cranston/Meston, Maple Ridge

Name: _____

Curricular Area: _____

Date Initiated: _____
Review Date: _____

Class Learning Outcomes • highlight appropriate objectives	Evaluation	As is	IS IT APPROPRIATE? with adapted goals/ expectations, presentation, evaluation, materials, assistance, or environment	Person Responsible	Individual Learning Outcomes (materials, criteria, review date)	Evaluation Comments (date achieved)

CRITICAL ACTIVITIES MATRIX
© Ives/Meston, Maple Ridge

Name: _____ Date: _____ Review Date: _____

CLASSROOM ACTIVITIES

INDIVIDUAL LEARNING OUTCOMES							

Annotated Bibliography of Classroom Resources

Picture Books (Kindergarten to Grade 7)

Blos, Joan. (Stephen Gammell, illus.). *Old Henry*. New York: Morrow, 1990. Henry gets tired of his neighbors bothering him about his beat-up old house. So he moves away. Now neither he nor the neighbors are happy.

THEMES: exclusion, accepting differences

Cannon, Janell. *Stellaluna*. New York: Harcourt Brace, 1999. A young fruit bat, separated from her mother, falls into a nest of birds. Stellaluna tries to adjust to eating bugs, sleeping at night and not hanging by her feet. She and her three bird friends learn to appreciate each other for their similarities and their differences.

_____. *Trupp: A Fuzzhead Tale*. New York: Harcourt Brace, 1998. A fuzzhead animal leaves his home to explore the world, finding out about friendship and danger.

THEMES: journey, belonging

Fleming, Virginia. (Floyd Cooper, illus.) *Be Good to Eddie Lee*. New York: Putnam and Grosset Group, 1993. When a young girl gets to know a boy with a disability, she discovers that what matters is not how you look, but what's in your heart.

THEMES: exclusion, friendship, diversity

Gregory, Nan. (Ron Lightburn, illus.). *How Smudge Came*. Red Deer, AB: Red Deer College Press. When her group home won't allow her to keep a puppy she finds, Cindy feels very alone. Then she finds she has friends after all.

THEMES: exclusion/inclusion, empathy, belonging

Madden, Don. *The Wartville Wizard*. New York: Aladdin Paperbacks, 1986. An old man gets tired of cleaning up everyone else's garbage. Then strange things begin to happen!

THEME: caring for our world

Muir, Stephen. (Mary Jane Muir, illus.) *Albert's Old Shoes*. Toronto: Stoddart, 1996. Albert gets so frustrated about everyone teasing him about his beat-up shoes that one day, in total frustration, he kicks a soccer ball an amazing distance. All of the children are wildly impressed.

THEMES: exclusion, belonging, peer pressure

Polacco, Patricia. *Babushka Baba Yaga*. New York: Putnam Publishing Group, 1993. Baba Yaga yearns to hold and care for a baby the way other older women enjoy their grandchildren. When she disguises herself as a visiting babushka, she is soon loved by a little boy. Then rumors poison her happiness.

THEMES: exclusion, belonging, rumors, not judging others

———. *The Keeping Quilt*. New York: Simon and Schuster Children's Books, 1988. A very special quilt, made from garments that have come from Russia, is passed down from generation to generation. This book looks at traditions that belong to groups of people and how things both change and stay the same over time.

THEMES: belonging, journeys, love, family

———. *Mrs. Katz and Tush*. New York: Bantam Little Rooster Book, 1992. Love grows between an old woman, a young boy, and a cat.

THEMES: belonging, love, friendship

———. *Thank You, Mr. Falker*. New York: Putnam Publishing Group, 1998. A young girl who has difficulty learning to read feels the stigma of being "different." Finally she meets a teacher who makes a big difference to her life.

THEMES: belonging, acceptance of self, learning journey

———. *The Trees of the Dancing Goats*. New York: Simon and Schuster Children's Books, 1996. During a time of sickness in a small community, a Jewish family helps their neighbors celebrate Christmas.

THEMES: friendship, inclusion, giving

Rylant, Cynthia. (Stephen Gammell, illus.) *The Relatives Came*. New York: Bradbury Press, 1985. Relatives help and love each other.

THEMES: caring, inclusion, belonging

Van Allsburg, Chris. *Just a Dream*. New York: Houghton Mifflin, 1990. A boy dreams of what will happen to the world if we do not take care of it.

THEMES: care for the world, personal journey to understanding

Wild, Margaret. (Julie Vivas, illus.) *The Very Best of Friends*. San Diego, CA: Harcourt Brace, 1989. When Jessie's husband, James, dies, Jessie becomes depressed and ignores his favorite pet, William. One day Jessie looks at William and is startled to see that he has become mean and lean. She begins to make amends and works toward becoming the very best of friends.

THEMES: belonging, exclusion

Williams, Margery. *The Velveteen Rabbit*. Philadelphia, PA: Running Press, 1981. If you belong, you become real. It does not matter what you look like; it's how you are treated that makes you real, makes you belong.

THEMES: belonging

Primary Books

Aliki. *Feelings*. New York: Morrow, 1986.

THEME: belonging

Bourgeois, Paulette, (Brenda Clark, illus.) *Franklin Goes to School*. Toronto: Kids Can Press, 1995.

THEMES: acceptance of self, learning journey

_____. *Franklin in the Dark*. Toronto: Kids Can Press, 1997.

THEME: learning journey

_____. *Franklin Plays the Game*. Toronto: Kids Can Press, 1995. Franklin discovers he needs practice and encouragement in order to improve.

THEME: learning journey

_____. *Franklin Ride a Bike*. Toronto: Kids Can Press, 1997. Franklin learns that some things are harder for some people than others, but that he can ride a bike if he keeps practising.

THEME: learning journey

_____. *Franklin's Secret Club*. Toronto: Kids Can Press, 1998.

THEMES: exclusion, belonging

Bunting, Eve. (Donald Carrick, illus.) *The Wednesday Surprise*. New York: Houghton Mifflin, 1990. A little girl teaches her grandmother to read.

THEMES: love, learning journey, sharing

Fitch, Sheree. (Darcia Labrosse, illus.) *If You Could Wear My Sneakers: A Book about Children's Rights*. Toronto: Doubleday, 1997. The author has created poems to help children understand the United Nations Rights of the Child.

THEMES: safety, belonging, acceptance

Fox, Mem. (Pamela Lofts, illus.) *Koala Lou*. New York: Harcourt Brace Jovanovich, 1988. A young Koala wonders about her busy mother's love and strives to win it back.

THEMES: unconditional love and acceptance, belonging

Gliori, Debi. *The Snow Lambs*. New York: Scholastic, 1996. A young boy worries when his dog does not return in a snowstorm. The illustrations depict the separate journeys of the dog and the boy on the same pages.

THEMES: caring, belonging, journey

Henkes, Kevin. *Chester's Way*. New York: Morrow, 1997. Chester learns that he can be friends with kids and learn from them whether they are like him or not.

THEMES: friendship, individual differences, inclusion

_____. *Lilly's Purple Plastic Purse*. New York: Greenwillow Books, 1996. This wonderful book is full of emotion, Lilly's feelings, and her ways of expressing them. Lilly learns a lot about herself and her teacher on a journey of the heart.

THEMES: belonging, feelings, journey

Joly, Fanny. *Mr. Fine, Porcupine*. San Francisco, CA: Chronicle Books, 1997.

THEME: friendship

Joose, Barbara. (Barbara Lavalle, illus.) *Mama, Do You Love Me?* San Francisco, CA: Chronicle Books, 1991. An Inuit mother reassures her daughter that though she may feel many emotions, she will still love her "forever and always."

THEMES: unconditional love, belonging

Kraus, Robert. (Jose Aruego, illus.) *Leo the Late Bloomer*. New York: HarperCollins Children's Books, 1998. Leo, a little tiger, has difficulty learning to read, write, talk, eat and draw, but given the gift of time he learns and blooms.

THEME: learning journey

LeBox, Annette. (Heather Holbrook, illus.) *Miss Rafferty's Rainbow Socks*. Toronto: HarperCollins, 1996. A friendship between an older woman and a young girl is portrayed in a magical way. Each of them gives up their most prized possession for the other.

THEMES: friendship, belonging, giving

Lester, Helen. (Lynn Munsinger, illus.) *A Porcupine Named Fluffy*. Boston: Houghton Mifflin, 1989. Fluffy is not fluffy no matter how hard he tries. He ventures out into the world and finds out that it is okay to be himself and even to laugh at himself.

THEME: acceptance of self

_____. *Tacky the Penguin*. Boston: Houghton Mifflin, 1988.

THEMES: diversity, belonging

_____. *Three Cheers for Tacky*. Boston: Houghton Mifflin, 1996. Tacky tries hard to be like the other penguins, but it is his uniqueness that saves the day!

THEMES: diversity, belonging

Lionni, Leo. *Swimmy*. New York: Random House, 1973. With Swimmy to help them, smaller fish form a shape that looks like one large fish and frighten their enemies away.

THEMES: belonging, working together

Lunn, Janet. (Kim LaFave, illus.) *Amos's Sweater*. Toronto: Groundwood, 1988. Amos is an old, cold sheep who is tired of giving up his wool. Aunt Hattie and Uncle Henry come to understand his point of view.

THEME: belonging

McBratney, Sam. (Anita Jeram, illus.) *Guess How Much I Love You*. Cambridge, MA: Candlewick Press, 1994.

THEMES: love, belonging

Munsch, Robert. (Eugenie Fernandes, illus.) *Ribbon Rescue*. Toronto: Scholastic Canada, 1999. Jillian gives away all of the ribbons from her traditional Mohawk dress to help others.

THEMES: belonging, giving

Plantos, Ted. (Heather Collins, illus.) *Heather Hits Her First Home Run*. Windsor, ON: Black Moss Press, 1989. Heather learns the value of perseverance.

THEMES: friendship, practice, and team spirit

Raschka, Christopher. *Yo! Yes?* New York: Orchard Books: 1993.

THEME: friendship

Rylant, Cynthia. (Arthur Howard, illus.) *Mr. Putter and Tabby Pour the Tea*. San Diego, CA: Harcourt Brace, 1994. Mr. Putter goes to the animal shelter to find a cat like him — old with thinning hair and creaking bones.

THEME: friendship

Simmie, Lois. (Cynthia Nugent, illus.) *Mister Got to Go: The Cat That Wouldn't Leave*. Red Deer, AB: Red Deer College Press, 1995. A stray cat becomes part of a hotel family.

THEME: belonging

Wild, Margaret. (Julie Vivas, illus.) *Our Granny*. New York: Ticknor and Fields, 1994.

THEMES: respecting diversity, belonging

Yorinks, Arthur (Mort Drucker, illus.) *Whitefish Will Rides Again!* New York: HarperCollins Children's Books, 1994.

THEME: non-violent conflict resolution

Intermediate Books

Boraks-Nemetz, Lillian. *The Old Brown Suitcase*. Brentwood Bay, BC: Ben-Simon Publications, 1994. Having survived the Second World War in Poland, a fourteen-year-old girl now living in Canada struggles with English, memories, new ways and customs.

THEMES: belonging, identity

Filipovic, Zlata. *Zlata's Diary: A Child's Life in Sarajevo*. New York: Viking Penguin, 1995. A young teenager struggles to make sense of life in war-torn Sarajevo in her diary. This true story was originally published by UNICEF.

THEMES: belonging, identity

Garrigue, Sheila. *The Eternal Spring of Mr. Ito*. New York: Simon and Schuster Children's Books, 1994. Evacuated from war-torn England during the Second World War, Sara is living with relatives in

Vancouver when the internment of Japanese begins. She tries to make sense of events.

THEMES: diversity, courage

Gleitzman, Morris. *Sticky Beak*. New York: Harcourt Brace Jovanovich, 1995. Rowena, who is mute, worries that the baby her father and new mother are expecting will be loved more than she is.

THEMES: belonging, family, change

Golenbock, Peter. (Paul Bacon, illus.) *Teammates*. New York: Harcourt Brace Jovanovich, 1990. This picture book talks about discrimination against blacks in America, focusing on the true baseball story of one white man who stood by his black teammate.

THEMES: exclusion, courage

Kidd, Diana. *Onion Tears*. New York: Orchard Books, 1991. A Vietnamese immigrant to Australia suffers so much rejection that she becomes mute.

THEMES: courage, belonging

Little, Jean. *From Anna*. New York: HarperCollins Children's Books, 1973. Anna suffers much teasing about her clumsiness, but after her family immigrates to a new land, her visual impairment is discovered. See also *Listen for the Singing*, which continues Anna's adventures.

THEMES: belonging, journey

Lowry, Lois. *Number the Stars*. Boston: Houghton Mifflin, 1995. Told from a Jewish girl's point of view, this story relates how the Danes saved many Jews around the time of the Second World War.

THEMES: courage, friendship

Matas, Carol. *Daniel's Story*. Richmond Hill, ON: Scholastic Canada, 1993. Daniel tells the story of his journey as a Jew from Frankfurt to Lodz to Auschwitz to Buchenwald.

THEME: journey

Paterson, Katherine. *The Great Gilly Hopkins*. New York: HarperCollins Children's Books, 1987. A bright obstreperous child in a loving foster home comes to understand love and family too late to stay where she is. She eventually goes to her grandmother's and learns where her "true grit" comes from.

THEMES: belonging, journey

Sadiq, Nazneen. *Camels Can Make You Homesick and Other Stories*. Toronto: James Lorimer, 1985. Five short stories of how new Canadians adjust to life in Canada.

THEMES: belonging, journey

Shyer, Marlene F. *Welcome Home, Jellybean*. New York: Simon and Schuster Children's Books, 1988. Neil's sister comes home from an institution, changing his life and the lives of his parents.

THEMES: belonging, caring

Smucker, Barbara. *Jacob's Little Giant*. Markham, ON: Penguin, 1987. A young boy, tired of being the "baby," grows through caring for a flock of Canada geese.

THEME: journey

Wilson, Budge. *A House Far from Home*. Richmond Hill, ON: Scholastic Canada, 1986.

THEMES: belonging, accepting diversity

_____. *Oliver's Wars*. Toronto: Stoddart, 1992. While his father serves in Saudi Arabia during the Gulf War, Oliver and his twin brother live with grandparents in Halifax. They deal with matters of safety, fear, a new school, and fitting in.

THEMES: belonging, courage

Voigt, Cynthia. *Homecoming*. New York: Fawcett, 1987. Four children, abandoned by their mother, learn to care for each other and stick together at all costs.

THEMES: belonging, journey

Music

Humphries, Pat. *Common Thread*. Wood Lake Books. Sheet Music.

THEME: belonging, community

Lea, Judy. *Too Much Work to Do*. Vancouver, BC: Tyrannosockus Productions, 1997. Compact Disk/Tape. Songs: "If You Care," "Every Little Thing," "If You Help Me"

THEME: belonging

Music for Little People. *Peace Is the World Smiling: A Peace Anthology for Families*. Redway, CA. Compact Disk. Songs: "Peace Is the World Smiling," "Hug the Earth," "Everybody Is Somebody," "Kids' Peace Song"

THEME: belonging, community

Raffi. *Bananaphone*. Vancouver, BC: Troubador Records, 1994. Compact Disk/Tape.

THEMES: care for the world, belonging

Rankin Family. *North Country*. EMI Music Canada. Compact Disk/Tape. Song: "We Will Rise Again"

THEME: community

Scott, Rick. *Philharmonic Fool*. Vancouver, BC: Jester Records, 1995. Compact Disk/Tape. Songs: "Grandma," "Angels Do," "You Make Me Happy"

THEMES: appreciating others, friendship

Thomas, Marlo, and Friends. *Free to Be You and Me*. Arista Records, 1983. Compact Disk/Tape.

THEMES: acceptance of self and others

Professional Bibliography

Allington, Richard L., and Sean A. Walmsley (ed.) *No Quick Fix: Rethinking Literacy Programs in America's Elementary Schools*. Newark, DE: IRA, 1995.

BCTF Case Studies. *Partners for Inclusion. No. 4. Peachland Primary and Elementary Schools*. Vancouver, B.C.: BCTF, 1994.

____. *Partners for Inclusion. No. 3. Sir Alexander Mackenzie Elementary School*. Vancouver, B.C.: BCTF, 1994.

Bellanca, James, and Robin Fogarty. *Catch Them Thinking: A Handbook of Classroom Strategies*. Arlington Heights, IL: IRI Skylight, 1986.

Brownlie, Faye, and Susan Close. *Beyond Chalk and Talk: Collaborative Strategies for the Middle and High School Years*. Markham, ON: Pembroke, 1992.

Brownlie, Faye, Susan Close, and Linda Wingren. *Reaching for Higher Thought: Reading, Writing, Thinking Strategies*. Edmonton, AB: Arnold, 1988.

____. *Tomorrow's Classroom Today: Strategies for Creating Active Readers, Writers, and Thinkers*. Markham, ON: Pembroke, 1990.

Brownlie, Faye, and Catherine Feniak. *Student Diversity: Addressing the Needs of All Learners in Inclusive Classroom Communities*: Markham, ON: Pembroke, 1998.

Cameron, Caren, Betty Tate, Daphne MacNaughton, and Colleen Politano. *Recognition without Rewards*. Winnipeg, MB: Peguis, 1997.

Cunningham, Patricia M., and Richard L. Allington. *Classrooms That Work: They Can All Read & Write*. Reading, MA: Addison-Wesley, 1998.

DeBoer, Anita. *The Art of Consulting*. Chicago: Arcturus Books, 1986.

____. *Working Together: The Art of Consulting and Communicating*. Longmont, CO: Sopris West, 1995.

Elias, Maurice, et al. *Promoting Social and Emotional Learning: Guidelines for Educators*. Baltimore, MD: ASCD, 1997.

Eyre, R., and L. Eyre. *Teaching Your Children Values*. New York: Simon and Schuster, 1993.

Fogarty, Robin, and Kay Opeka. *Start Them Thinking: A Handbook of Strategies for the Early Years*. Arlington Heights, IL: IRI Skylight, 1988.

Goleman, Daniel. *Emotional Intelligence*. New York: Bantam, 1995.

Gregory, Kathleen, Caren Cameron, and Anne Davis. *Setting and Using Criteria*. Boothbay, ME: Connections Pub., 1997.

Keefe, Charlotte Hendrick. *Label-Free Learning: Supporting Learners with Disabilities*. York, ME: Stenhouse, 1996.

Hingsburger, David. *Eye Opener*. Vancouver, B.C.: Family Support Institute Press, 1993.

Jensen, Eric. *Teaching with the Brain in Mind*. Baltimore, MD: ASCD, 1998.

Knox, Gerald. *Vegetables, Herbs and Fruit*. Des Moines, IA: Better Homes and Gardens, 1988.

Lajoie, Gerald. *Take Action against Bullying*. Coquitlam, B.C.: Bully B'ware Productions, 1997.

Lang, Greg, and Chris Berberich. *All Children Are Special: Creating an Inclusive Classroom*. York, ME: Stenhouse, 1995.

Leach, Penelope. *Children First: What Society Must Do — and Is Not Doing — for Children Today*. London, U.K.: Vintage Books, 1994.

Maslow, A. H. *Toward a Psychology of Being* (3rd ed.). New York: Wiley, 1998.

McGinnis, Ellen, and Arnold P. Goldstein. *Skillstreaming in Early Childhood: Teaching Prosocial Skills to the Preschool and Kindergarten Child*. Champaign, IL: Research Press, 1990.

____. *Skillstreaming the Elementary School Child: New Strategies and Perspectives for Teaching Prosocial Skills* (rev. ed.). Champaign, IL: Research Press, 1997.

Perske, Robert. *Circle of Friends*. Burlington, ON: Welch Pub., 1988.

Roller, Cathy M. *So . . . What's a Tutor to Do?* Newark, DE: IRA, 1998.

Santa, Carol Minnick. *Project CRISS*. Dubuque, IA: Kendall/Hunt Publishing, 1996.

Stainback, S., and W. Stainback. (ed.) *Support Networks for Inclusive Schooling*. Baltimore, Maryland: Paul H. Brookes Publishing, 1990.

Villa, R., and J. Thousand. *Creating an Inclusive School*. Baltimore, MD: ASCD, 1995.

Index